MANAGEMENT DEVELOPMENT STRATEGY IN THE FINANCIAL SECTOR

Management Development Strategy in the Financial Sector

Malcolm Higgs

MACMILLAN
PRESS

First published 1988

Published by
THE MACMILLAN PRESS LTD
Houndmills, Basingstoke, Hampshire RG21 2XS
and London
Companies and representatives
throughout the world

Typeset by Wessex Typesetters
(Division of The Eastern Press Ltd)
Frome, Somerset

Printed in Hong Kong

British Library Cataloguing in Publication Data
Higgs, Malcolm
Management development strategy in the
financial sector.
1. Financial institutions—Employees
—Training of 2. Management—Study
and teaching 3. Career development
I. Title
658.4′07124   HD8039.1326
ISBN 0–333–43407–2

To Jacki, Paul and Katie

Contents

A review of the main considerations which need to be
taken into account in the formulation of an effective
management development strategy. Outline of a
framework for planning a development strategy.

An examination of current thinking and practice in
relation to management development strategy in the
financial sector. Illustrations of changes that are taking
place and identification of common trends and
developments.

A review of the methods of management development
being used in the financial sector. An indication of the
increasing range of methods being employed and the
need to consider methods well beyond the 'traditional'
confines of training and education.

Establishing that effective management development
requires an integrated strategy which brings a range of
personnel systems together to achieve development
objectives. Illustrations of situations where such an
integrated approach is being effectively implemented.

An examination of changing roles and responsibilities
associated with new approaches to management
development strategy. Illustrations of how personnel
and management development accountabilities and
roles are being handled in organisations implementing
a more business-oriented approach to management
development.

Preface

In my work in the field of management development, I was, for many years, frustrated by the lack of impact which the process appeared to have within the companies for which I worked.

Reflecting on this, it occurred to me that what I called management development was, in fact, no more than management training and education. Frequently I had built these programmes on an academic, or idealised, view of the nature of managerial jobs and their working environments. This realisation led to a fundamental rethinking of my views on the nature and function of management development. I concluded that management development needs to be seen as an integral part of business strategy, if it is to have any significant impact on business performance. It has to be rooted in the reality of the business environment and to be far broader in its focus than the traditional combination of management training, education and succession planning.

Having arrived at this conclusion it became necessary to sell the concept to senior management. The experience of doing this, in a number of organisations, was frequently a frustrating one. However, after a number of years it became apparent that the concept was much more readily 'bought' in situations where the organisation was faced with major changes in its business environment, or significant changes in business strategy.

Over the last few years this pattern has been clear in the financial sector. I have encountered an increasing level of interest in management development by senior management. There has appeared a growing recognition of a need to convert the phrase 'people are important to our business' into practice. This shift in thinking clearly results from the increasing levels of uncertainty and challenge emanating from the rapid, and far-reaching, changes taking place in the sector.

The change in my own views as a management development practitioner, combined with the change in senior management perceptions, played an important part in giving rise to producing this book. It seemed both useful and necessary to encapture and articulate these changes in thinking, and to examine management development strategies which are appropriate for organisations in the new, and still volatile and highly competitive, financial sector environment.

The changes described were, however, only one part of the process which led to this book. The other major driving force resulted from numerous discussions I had with people responsible for management development within financial organisations. Many of these people were clearly articulating the need for fundamental changes in management development strategy. These needs were seen as pressing, if their organisations were to survive in a difficult climate. At the same time many of those I spoke to felt frustrated by their organisations' reluctance to take on board the concept of management development becoming an integrated part of the business planning process. This provided the final stimulus necessary to put pen to paper in the hope that the messages could be widely disseminated, and support others' efforts to bring about a necessary change in thinking.

Many of the people I have discussed management development strategy with have provided valuable insights into, and views on, the process of development in financial organisations. Of all of those I have spoken to, I am particularly grateful to Melvyn Howell (Management Development Manager, Midland Bank) and Anika Sandström (Director, Wallenberg Institute of Skandinaviska Enskilda Banken) for the insights which they provided into both the development process, and the way in which banks need to respond to changes in their markets.

Having reached the decision to write a book, which encapsulated the need for a change in management development thinking in the financial sector, I faced the problem of deciding how to approach the topic. Although I had my own views and experience (based on consulting with financial sector organisations) to draw on, I was keen to test them out and produce a picture showing current thinking and practice within organisations. I was also keen to examine the thinking and practice from the viewpoint of both senior management and management development practitioners. This inevitably led to the conclusion that I would need to talk to people in a range of organisations in the sector.

In selecting organisations to approach I resisted the temptation to adopt an 'Excellence' format. The aim was to obtain views from a reasonable cross-section of organisations which would, to an extent, reflect the wide diversity of organisations operating within the sector.

The avoidance of an 'Excellence' format by no means implies that the companies selected are not excellent ones. Clearly many of them are. The framework adopted was chosen in order to avoid any implication that there is only one approach to effective management development; also to establish that, although practice may vary widely, there are a number of common threads in thinking on development strategy.

I am very grateful to all of those who contributed to the discussions and freely gave up much time to them. As there were so many involved I have acknowledged their contribution separately. However, I would, at this stage, particularly like to thank Derek Day, of Alexander Howden Management Services, who spent many hours discussing not only his organisation's strategy, but also the overall picture in the financial sector and the approach to developing the book.

I must also thank my wife, Jacki, who undertook the mammoth task of typing the manuscript. More importantly she provided critical comment, support, encouragement and regular reminders of the need to complete the task!

I hope that the result of the time invested, by all concerned, in producing this book is a view of management development strategy which will stimulate the thinking of both senior management and management development practitioners in the financial sector. Changes in development strategy and practice are needed in the sector. I am convinced that if these changes are made, they will contribute to the development of stronger and more effectively managed organisations, which will be able to perform well in a difficult and volatile market.

London MALCOLM HIGGS

Acknowledgements

I would like to acknowledge the help provided by the following people, in taking time to discuss management development practice in both their organisations and the financial sector in general. I would also like to thank them, and their organisations for allowing me to quote their views and practices in this book.

Peter Birch, Chief Executive, Abbey National Building Society

Dennis Brockwell, Assistant General Manager, Field Operations, Nationwide Building Society

Harry Broomhead, Group Personnel Manager, Royal Insurance Group plc

Garrett Bouton, Managing Director and Chief Executive, Scandinavian Bank Group plc

Brian Chandler, Director of Training, Arthur Young

Derek Day, Managing Director, Alexander Howden Management and Data Services Limited

Dr Wilfried Guth, Member of the Board of Managing Directors, Deutsche Bank A G

Jeffrey Hernu, Director, Barclays de Zoette Wedd

John Horner, Corporate Planning Manager, Lombard Continental Insurance plc

Melvyn Howell, Manager, Management Development, Retail Division, Midland Bank plc

Donald Kirkham, Chief Executive, Woolwich Equitable Building Society

Crawford Laughlan, General Manager, Administration, Halifax Building Society

Malcolm Parker, Training Director, Citicorp Investment Bank

Peter Rowe, Chief Manager, Training Co-ordination, Lloyds Bank plc

Peter Russell, Training and Development Manager, Allied Dunbar Assurance plc

Jack Rutley, Management Development Manager, Nationwide Building Society

David Salmon, Secretary (Education and Training), Chartered Insurance Institute

John Skae, General Manager, Group Resources, Legal and General
Group plc
David Woodward, Personnel Director, Scandinavian Bank Group
plc

I would also like to thank the following journals for giving their
permission to quote from articles:

Personnel Management
Training and Development
Journal of European Industrial Training

M. H.

1 The Challenge of Change

The financial sector is in the midst of an unprecedented period of change. The fundamental nature of much of this change has led to it being described as the Financial Services Revolution. This phrase implies that the implications for the financial sector are as significant as those faced in manufacturing during the Industrial Revolution.

Whether the general implications are as significant or not, it is clear that the structure and nature of the financial sector is changing significantly. The way in which individual businesses within the sector are structured and managed is also changing. This is giving rise to a perceived need for different skills on the part of those managing the businesses.

In this climate of change companies are seeking strategies which will ensure their survival and continued growth. Those organisations that are to succeed will have to formulate a clear and effective strategy for developing managers able to operate effectively in such an environment.

This book sets out to examine strategies for successfully developing managers who will be able to contribute to a company's survival in the volatile markets in which financial organisations now operate.

The main questions examined in the book are:

● What are the main issues associated with the changes in the sector?

● What are the implications of these issues in terms of the skills and talents required to effectively manage businesses?

● To what extent can existing approaches to management development provide organisations with the managers they will need?

● What changes in management development strategy are being contemplated and implemented in the sector?

● How can a management development strategy, which will meet the current and future needs of a financial sector business, be evolved and implemented?

● What are the main components of a successful strategy?

1

The starting point for examining these questions is to examine the main changes in the sector and their implications. This is not the cue to launch into a detailed description of changes in legislation and practice. However, in order to review management development strategies, it is useful to have a clear picture of the context in which they have to be implemented.

The nature and implications of the changes in the sector are somewhat different for the key constituent business areas. To review the environment the sector has been divided into:

● Banks, stockbrokers and stockjobbers
● Building societies
● Insurance organisations

In many ways one of the results of the changes is that these divisions are becoming increasingly arbitrary. In the words of Donald Kirkham (Chief Executive of the Woolwich Equitable Building Society):

> The sector deals in one product. Money. It is an extremely homogenous product.

Although the way in which organisations are developing tends to underpin this statement, their starting points and the nature of the changes being faced are different. These differences are summarised in the following pages.

BANKS, STOCKBROKERS AND STOCKJOBBERS

The grouping of banks with stockbrokers and stockjobbers is in itself reflecting one of the major changes affecting this part of the financial sector. 'Big Bang' (1986) has formalised a process of integrating a range of financial services aimed at corporate customers and high-net-worth individuals. The change in Stock Exchange regulations has allowed UK and overseas banks to invest in its member firms and to become members themselves. In practice this has now happened and the markets for securities has seen the arrival of new entrants and significant new groupings of banking, broking and jobbing organisations.

'Big Bang' has also resulted in a fundamental change in the way in which securities are bought and sold. Market making and selling activities may now take place under the umbrella of one company (the arrangement referred to as 'dual capacity'). Thus organisations are now operating in the markets which combine banking, stockbroking and stockjobbing units.

One further major change has occurred in this market. This is the ending of the fixed commissions on the sale and purchase of securities. Commission rates are now negotiable.

The post-'Big Bang' market is, therefore, one in which the number, size and structure of the players has changed dramatically, as have the terms on which they do business. Overall it is a market in which competition is fierce.

The extent to which the market has been opened up is illustrated by the changes in the market in gilt-edged stock. The Bank of England no longer deals with a market dominated by two jobbing firms. Instead it now deals with 29 primary dealers!

The changes in Stock Exchange regulations and practice which is referred to as 'Big Bang' has, in reality, been no more than the alteration to formal structures to enable the UK market to adapt to the pressures resulting from a number of major international trends. These trends may be summarised as:

(a) Foreign competition

The ending of exchange controls in 1979 removed the barrier between domestic and international capital markets. This led to increasing competition for business and resulted in investors becoming more conscious of the need to obtain value for money, both in terms of charges and the service offered.

(b) Information technology

The explosive pace of development of information technology has broken down the barriers between individual financial markets. Participants in major markets have simultaneous access to information, combined with the ability to execute trading electronically. This facility has led to global 24-hour trading in many financial instruments.

(c) Securitisation of debt

The way in which large corporations can raise money to meet their financial needs has been changing. A whole range of instruments have been developed which provide cheaper alternatives to taking bank credit.

Corporations can raise money through commercial paper, share issue and a range of long- and short-term instruments. Essentially debt is becoming readily interchangeable, flowing through a whole range of instruments, and readily convertible from one currency to another.

(d) Growth of institutional investors

During the last 20 years in the UK, the major institutional investors have become increasingly significant. Their holdings in the market have grown to a level where they have been able to exert pressure for change in market regulations and created the need for jobbers to merge to have a sufficient capital base to carry inventories to meet their requirements.

These are the trends in international markets underlying 'Big Bang'. The change in regulations has provided the large commercial banks (British, American and European) with the opportunity to gain access to the securities markets by acquiring under-capitalised stockbrokers and jobbers. The new organisations have capital bases, enabling them to compete effectively, combined with expanded distribution power to enable them to handle security-based, as well as other more traditional, financial instruments.

It is clear that the market place is becoming highly competitive. The consumer will certainly benefit from this. For the players, however, there is an increasing need to think in terms of survival strategies. Many of the old divisions between particular organisations, based on product specialisation or market segmentation, are disappearing. It is widely felt that the market will polarise splitting between:

● A small number of top international financial groupings providing wholesale funding for large corporations and investment services for very rich individuals.

● 'Boutique' organisations providing highly-discounted, 'no frills' services to the smaller and middle sections of the market.

The customers themselves are becoming increasingly sophisticated and will be demanding higher levels of, and more individually tailored, services.

The speed of development of products to meet customer needs is increasing and, given the rapid flow of information, combined with the dominance of large organisations, could well soon result in the products offered by competitors being virtually indistinguishable.

Developing a strategy for survival in such a difficult market calls for organisations to make a fundamental reappraisal of their role in providing financial services. People with the skills necessary to contribute to survival and success in such an environment are at a premium already. The indications are that, as competition for business escalates, so will the competition for skilled people.

Organisations appear to be responding to these challenges in one of two ways. Those organisations at the smaller end of the market are increasingly looking at the development of 'niche' strategies. These are based on exploitation of customer base, geographic or market sector advantages. The larger organisations are looking to reorganise in order to effectively compete across a whole range of products, and re-examining the way in which they market and manage customer relationships.

Malcolm Parker (Training Director, Citicorp Investment Bank) sums up the situation as follows:

> The changes in the markets are forcing organisational change. Citicorp are moving to integrate corporate banking and investment banking activities. The investment bank will use the corporate banking distribution channels.

He goes on:

> The opportunity for competitive advantages on a product basis is fast disappearing. All competitors are essentially doing the same things. To succeed there is a need to get closer to the customer and to understand their needs better than has traditionally been the case.

A number of key players are looking to change to a financial institution which is fully equipped to engineer solutions which will enable clients to finance themselves in the most efficient, flexible, innovative and sophisticated way.

Innovation will play a key role in securing temporary competitive advantage, but products will certainly have a shorter life cycle.

The financial engineering approach, combined with greater product innovation, will feature in most large banks. To provide a flexible, responsive and innovative service, those organisations who have acquired brokers and jobbers will need to succeed in achieving effective integration of these businesses with their corporate and investment banking activities.

For these organisations, integration is the key to success. Integration needs to provide an effective problem-solving capacity for their customers. Rather than look at the organisation in traditional functional terms the design should provide:

Marketing teams.   These teams will manage customer relationships, identify needs and maintain a dialogue with the customers.

Problem solvers.   Professional teams of specialists with responsibility for developing solutions to meet customer needs.

Securities specialists.   Those with a clear understanding of market appetites, trends and opportunities, providing a link and facility to effectively place securitised issues used to meet customer needs.

For the corporate sector of the market the position is one of:

● Increasingly fierce competition
● A need for an expanded product range
● Greater complexity in products
● A move to a responsive customer focus
● Shorter product life cycles
● More volatile markets
● Increasing destandardisation of products
● Greater product innovation
● A fundamental change in the nature and structure of the key organisations

The last point may be expanded to further illustrate the fundamental nature of the changes taking place. It is possible, given the opening up of entry to the markets, that future key players will not even be banks. There is no barrier to large organisations, such as IBM, becoming players. Given their increasing sophistication in financial management, and their tendency to view treasury management as a real contributor to profits, this scenario is by no means far-fetched.

The changes outlined are not merely a one-off disruption in an otherwise stable market. Change and volatility are here to say.

Garrett Bouton (Chief Executive of Scandinavian Bank) clearly summarised the situation in a talk given at the International Conference on Bank Training in April 1986:

Traditionally, banks have tended to react to external change by means of relatively slow incremental change in their own organisation. The nature and extent of the change taking place in our industry today must call into question the continuation of an incremental change system. The need is for radical change. Increasingly we shall have to be able to respond rapidly to significant shifts in the external environment. This need implies a requirement to move from logical, quantitative approaches to problem-solving to a more qualitative approach.

RETAIL BANKING

The degree of change in the corporate banking sector has been well publicised and commented on in connection with 'Big Bang'. The retail sector, however, is also facing up to the need for radical change.

For many years the major retail banks have, through their branch network, neglected the personal banking sector. The main emphasis has been on developing corporate clients. However, the banks have suffered a loss of market share in the retail sector, with building societies aggressively competing for personal deposits.

The recent legislation, affecting personal finances, has tended to be based upon fiscal neutrality in terms of competitive advantage between banks, life assurers and building societies.

Given large branch networks, which are expensive to operate, growth in competition, and often poor experience in lending (particularly in international and sovereign risk finance), the banks have re-examined the retail sector. It has been found to be a potentially rewarding area upon which to focus.

The UK-based retail banks have found that competition is coming from foreign banks as well as the traditional financial sector competitors.

The advances in technology of money transmission (particularly the cash dispensing (ATM) networks) has called into question the role of the branches. Given the high costs of maintaining a branch network, the need to actively use branches for marketing and cross-selling products has emerged as a major issue. The role of the branch manager is rapidly shifting from that of a lender and administrator to that of a marketeer.

Competition is growing for investment, lending and money transmission products. Traditional segmentation with groups serving each segment, has disappeared. Building societies are offering money transmission, insurers are offering broader investment products and mortgages.

All of this is taking place against a background which is enhancing consumer financial awareness and stimulating an appetite for a wider range of investment options (for example, the UK government's privatisation programme has been positioned as a way of encouraging wider share ownership).

As a result of these trends, retail banking is faced with a need to provide, and actively market, a wider range of products. The differentiation between products and organisations in this sector is diminishing and, as with the corporate sector, there is a clearly-emerging need to get closer to the customer.

The extension of the product range to encompass new services is taking banks into areas in which they do not traditionally have expertise, and are not seen as being key providers of services, for example, life assurance and mortgages. This is lending to a re-examination of the roles of managers, structures and marketing strategies.

Retail banks will be aiming at a one-stop financial services distribution network. The range of services already encompasses:

● Money transmission
● Personal lending
● Mortgages
● Personal insurances
● Savings and investment

The move into the mortgage market has been dramatic. The market is one which offers a high level of security and reasonable return on capital employed. Banks have been successful in moving into this traditional building society market. The market is particularly important as it provides access to a range of housing-related financial services. A number of banks have even moved into the estate agency business as part of their strategy for developing this market.

In the provision of insurance services, banks are primarily playing an intermediary role. However, given the trend away from traditional roles, there is no reason why this role should not also alter. Indeed, the Royal Bank of Scotland already provides motor insurance as an insurer rather than intermediary.

Distribution is a major issue in the retail sector. The need to get closer to the customer has already led the major banks to re-examine, and in many cases change, the layout of their branches and opening hours. The aim here is to move away from the bank having an image associated with money transmission and traditional lending and towards being a financial services retail outlet. Many banks are also looking to establish outlets within shops as part of the financial services retail strategy.

Although many of the changes have been driven by competition, there is no doubt that technology has, and will continue to be, a major force for change. The rapid access to information, combined with the ability to execute deals and other business electronically will certainly play a major role in the development of selling shares through the branch network and providing insurance services.

In general banks are looking to move away from a dependence on loan-related income and to move towards obtaining a greater contribution from fee-related income.

Overall the general picture in retail banking sector is one of:

- Increasing competition
- Expanded, and rapidly changing, product ranges
- Dealing with more financially aware and sophisticated customers
- Moving to a customer focus
- Shorter product life cycles
- Greater emphasis on marketing and selling

Innovation will be a key to success in this environment. The rate of change will certainly continue, if not escalate. Branch managers will need to be able to change to effectively operate in this environment, and will be very clearly in a front line position.

BUILDING SOCIETIES

Building societies are organisations peculiar to the UK. Their roots lay in mutual 'clubs', owned by investors and having the simple purpose of expanding home ownership through the encouragement of thrift.

The sector has enjoyed dramatic growth in terms of its share of the personal savings market and its dominance in the provision of housing finance through mortgages.

Until some five or six years ago, the sector was in a protected and comfortable position. The 'movement', as it was known, essentially operated as a cartel, fixing mortgage and investment rates.

As mutuals the economics of the business was relatively simple. Once the rate, which was felt necessary to attract investors, had been established, the lending rate could be calculated by adding management expenses and margins to the rate offered to depositors.

The 'cartel', and lack of competition from other providers of mortgages, resulted in comfortable margins between investor and mortgage rates.

Building societies essentially were two product businesses with a dominant market share. Traditionally they had 50 per cent of the personal liquid assets market. Their share of the personal savings market grew, largely at the expense of the retail banks. This arose in part because of the banks' lack of emphasis on the retail sector, and in part due to their ability to offer attractive rates to savers resulting from their ability to 'fix' mortgage rates.

The government's actions, in pursuit of the policy of fiscal neutrality in competition for personal financial services, have resulted in societies losing a number of competitive advantages. In addition the 'cartel' has ceased to operate. These combined moves have opened up the sector to an enormous degree of competition. Whilst the savings market has always been competitive, the attractiveness of mortgage lending has brought banks (and indeed insurers) aggressively into this market. At the same time competition between societies escalated rapidly.

The result of new entrants and increased competition has been an upward pressure on rates paid to savers, combined with a downward pressure on rates charged to borrowers. This has narrowed societies' margins considerably and led to pressures to improve the effectiveness of their management. It has also led to a reappraisal of their traditional approach to achieving growth by expansion of branch networks. The economics of branch operations is being re-examined and, as with retail banking, a need to view them as retail financial services outlets is emerging.

An indication of the extent of the pressure on rates is provided by the shift in balance in types of investment account. Five to six years ago 90 per cent of investment accounts were ordinary share accounts.

Since then the balance has shifted to one where 75 per cent of accounts are higher interest ones. On the mortgage side, in August 1985 societies abandoned their higher rate differential for large mortgages and in February 1986 they abandoned their higher rate for endowment mortgages.

The pressures resulting from increased competition have led the societies to re-examine their role. In essence they saw the way forward requiring a movement towards providing a wider range of financial services. Achieving this entailed being freed from the tight legislative framework governing their activities.

Given the government's moves to deregulate the financial sector, the societies effectively took the initiative and drafted a paper which outlined the way in which legislation governing them should be changed. New legislation should recognise changes in the financial markets and enable them to complete effectively. These proposals were largely incorporated in to the Building Societies Act which came into force in January 1987. In introducing the legislation Nigel Lawson, Chancellor of the Exchequer, indicated that its central theme was to:

> further encourage home ownership and allow for fuller and freer competition in the provision of financial services.

The legislation provides a basis for moving a building society from a simple business, uncluttered by corporate customers, towards being one virtually indistinguishable from a retail bank.

The provisions of the legislation are extensive and detailed. However the key areas in which societies may well be operating as a result of the changes may be summarised as:

- Provision of personal loans
- Issue of cheque guarantee cards
- Provision of overdraft facilities
- Issuing credit or charge cards
- Joining cheque-clearing schemes
- Provision of full money transmission services
- Operating overseas (within the European Economic Community (EEC))
- Operating estate agency businesses
- Purchasing subsidiary companies for cash
- Provision of insurance services
- Sale of stocks and shares

The above list shows how closely societies will move towards being like a retail bank. It will take time for societies to be able to effectively offer all of these services. Crawford Laughlan (General Manager of the Halifax Building Society) represented the views of many in saying:

> There is so much in the new building society legislation, that societies will not be able to offer all of the potential services from day one.

In addition to coping with delivering a new range of products, societies face the challenge of changing their scope and style without losing the competitive advantage of their approachable and friendly public image.

One further important provision in the legislation is that enabling societies to demutualise and reform as a public limited company. Currently such provisions are tightly limited in order to prevent societies being snapped up by predators (particularly overseas banks seeking a retail network in the UK).

The ability to demutualise is seen as critical to survival by a number of societies. Currently they will only be able to make acquisitions, grow, expand and diversify by using cash. Even given the large reserves of the major societies, this would be difficult to do on a significant scale. Formation as a plc would enable acquisitions and funding for expansion to be under-pinned by the company's paper, rather than cash. Some societies see tight limitations on demutualisation as a major constraint which will inhibit full competition with other organisations in the sector.

The changes occurring are fundamental. Building societies have evolved from organisations with firm and clear value systems incorporating strong social values and commitment. Current changes are being responded to by societies in two distinct ways. One response is to whole-heartedly accept the change in direction and push actively to be able to compete freely as any other financial sector organisation. The other response is to acknowledge the need for change, but to adhere to traditional values and views on mission and to, in fact, perceive these as providing a competitive advantage within the segment of the retail sector historically serviced by the societies.

Competition and provision of an extended range of services are clearly key issues to be addressed by the building society sector.

Competition is squeezing margins and increasing the cost of funds from the traditional retail base. This has brought about another significant change in the way societies operate. Demands for mortgages have been satisfied by raising funds from investors. The growth and promotion of home ownership in the UK has fuelled the demand for mortgages. Increased costs of retail funds would normally have resulted in a shortfall leading to mortgage queues. However, to prevent loss of mortgage leading to competitors, and to improve margins, the societies have raised funds in the wholesale markets. This has given rise to a need for new treasury management skills to be brought into the societies.

Pressures on margins will force societies to look carefully at their management costs. It will also increase their need to derive income from non-mortgage sources. This is yet another pressure leading to extension of services and the need for branches to actively develop fee-earning services such as insurance. Like retail banks, they will have to review the role of branch managers and become far more selling-oriented.

Over many years there have been frequent mergers of societies. These have been driven by needs to extend branch networks and to form merged societies of a size capable to taking advantage of the benefits of technology. This merger process is likely to continue and lead to a polarisation of the market with a small number of national, very large societies at one extreme and a number of small societies, serving specific niches, at the other.

Overall the societies face:

● Increasing competition
● An increasing need to improve the productivity and marketing performance of the branch network
● Requirements for increased efficiency
● Developing and managing an extended and more complex range of products and services

The pressures for change in this sector were highlighted by Donald Kirkham of the Woolwich:

> The impact of deregulation and growth in competition are critical issues for building societies. The societies traditionally operated in a specialised field and controlled a massive empire. There is now a need to defend this empire. Successful societies will need to move into a position of defenders with a crusading zeal.

Crawford Laughlan of the Halifax summarises the key challenges being faced by the societies, as:

The challenges facing building societies are to provide all of the facilities that customers want and to retain their share of the mortgage lending market.

THE INSURANCE SECTOR

It is very difficult to look on insurance organisations as being a homogeneous group. This part of the financial sector splits into two major divisions, which are Life Assurance and General Insurance. The general insurance sector divides essentially into the corporate market and personal lines or domestic market. Some of the large composite offices encompass operations in all of these markets. Overlaid on these divisions are the insurance brokers who provide an intermediary service between the insurers and customers.

It is not my intention to go into a detailed analysis of the structure of this sector. However, it is useful to identify separately the major trends and issues associated with life assurers, general insurers and intermediaries.

Life assurance

The life assurance offices are the sub-group within this sector most readily aligned with the analysis of trends and issues facing banks and building societies.

For many years now life assurance companies have been emphasising and promoting investment rather than protection products. Their business has also been actively linked with the provisions of mortgages through using endowment policies as a means of repaying mortgage capital.

The focus on investment products has been underlined by the growth and proliferation of unit-linked policies.

Their target market for business overlaps with banks and building societies, although their products are providing a basis for medium-to long-term investment.

The life assurance industry is no stranger to competition. Levels of competition between offices has been growing steadily over the last 20 years, particularly since Abbey Life and Hambro Life entered the market with aggressive and successful sales driven strategies.

The legislative trend towards fiscal neutrality has certainly been felt by the life offices. The abolition of life assurance premium tax relief had a major impact on business.

Over the last 10 years the degree of innovation in products has moved life assurers more firmly into the investment area. The trend is for them to see themselves more clearly as being in the financial services business.

Increasingly offices are marketing unit trusts, becoming direct providers of domestic mortgages and marketing single premium investment bonds.

Some offices are taking this process further by linking with other organisations to provide further services. For example, Irish Life have linked with Western Trust and Savings to provide a cheque book, personal loan and cash card facility linked to their core unit-linked investment products.

The movement into full competition with other financial organisations is highlighted by the example of Prudential Assurance's strategy of acquisition of estate agents.

Although competing with banks and building societies, life offices also have a relationship with them as suppliers of business. Both banks and building societies act as intermediaries for life offices, selling their products to their own customers.

The level of competition within the industry has resulted in more life offices becoming sales driven and investing resources in developing new products.

Again consumers are becoming more sophisticated and knowledgeable. This is resulting in an increasing need to develop flexible and adaptable products. Such developments lead to changes in support and administrative services both at the time of sale and during the currency of the contracts.

The Financial Services Act, is having, and will continue to have, a major impact on the life industry. The drive for investor protection underlying the legislation has impacted on life offices in giving quotations for business. In preparing quotes, anticipated yields and expenses have set limits which may not be exceeded. This, combined with a race to compete across a full product range, will reduce significantly product differentiation between offices. As a result there will be increased emphasis on the salesforce developing an effective relationship with customers, and offices being flexible and adaptable in responding to customer needs.

The major impact of the Financial Services legislation will be on the way life assurance is sold to the public. The effect of the legislation will be to impose strict conditions on anyone wishing to act as an independent intermediary. The aim is to ensure that the public are provided with truly independent advice.

This is expected to have a dramatic effect on the structure of the market. The large national brokers will remain independent, as will a number of the 'high street chains'. However, many of the small- and medium-sized firms will cease to operate as brokers and either become salesmen or representatives for a single life office.

Many life offices do an extensive amount of business through the small- and medium-sized brokers. If these offices are to continue to survive, they will have to change their approach and either employ salesmen selling direct to the public or find alternative means of distribution. This will result in significant changes in the way in which these offices are organised and managed.

Distribution is a major issue for most life offices. Those with both direct and broker sales forces will need to review the balance of effort and possibly their structure and management approach. Increasingly offices are considering new means of marketing and distribution, including direct mail and joint ventures with other financial organisations. This latter route will be particularly important if the range of financial services provided is to be extended.

General insurance

(a) *Corporate business*
The corporate general insurance market is subject to pressures for change of a different nature to other parts of the financial sector. This market is characterised by underwriting cycles which have a dramatic impact on profitability and performance.

When underwriting results are good, more competitors are seeking business. This has the impact of pushing rates down. This in turn leads to the companies making underwriting losses. After a period of loss, the level of competition reduces and rates increase until a return to profitability is seen. The cycle is then repeated.

This is a very simplistic picture of the market. However, the down part of the cycle has recently been lasting for a long time. Due to high interest rates some offices have written business to either retain market share or acquire premium for investment. They have lived with underwriting losses as long as they have been able to show a trading profit.

Although there are signs that rates are hardening, most general insurers have had to face up to poor results over an extended period. This has placed pressure on costs and led to reviews of how the offices are organised and managed. The unpredictability of the underwriting cycles has meant that planning has become more difficult and managers have had to cope with a volatile and ambiguous environment.

(b) *Personal lines business*
The retail end of the general insurance market has also been hit by poor results due to high claim costs.

This, however, is the high volume area of the business and, in order to manage in difficult markets, companies have looked at means of reducing both processing and distribution costs.

The high volume nature of the business has meant that companies have been able to take advantage of technology to improve processing efficiency.

In terms of distribution, in many cases technology has caused the offices problems. Brokers have ready access to rates through systems such as Quotel. This has resulted in the public regularly being advised to switch insurers, in order to minimise increases in premiums. This has been most marked in the field of motor insurance. The high volatility resulting from regular switching of insurers has increased the costs of this business. Insurers have found a greater degree of stability of business when customers deal directly with them. This has resulted in increased interest in direct marketing of personal lines business.

Overall the retail side of general insurance is becoming increasingly marketing driven.

It is in the area of personal lines business that general insurers encounter banks and building societies. Currently their relationship is one of co-operation rather than competition. The banks and building societies are in an intermediary role rather than being direct providers of cover. Insurers will increasingly be exploring possibilities of using banks and building societies as distribution channels. This will have the advantage of providing high volume business which can be efficiently processed at manageable costs.

Relationships with banks may, however, change if many follow the example of the Royal Bank of Scotland, which is providing motor insurance as a direct insurer rather than as an intermediary. The growth of this trend would significantly increase the level of competition in this market.

Insurance brokers

The insurance broking market is dominated by a relatively small number of large, national brokers. Remaining broking organisations are either specialist offices, operating in the corporate market, or small- and medium-sized, locally-based, broking firms. The small- and medium-sized firms who deal with a significant amount of life business are likely to be dramatically affected by the Financial Services legislation (as outlined in the section on life assurance).

The specialist firms tend to be largely family firms who will continue to operate effectively in their specific niche, or ultimately be absorbed into the large, national firms.

The large, national firms have tended to grow by a process of merger and acquisition. These firms have grown from smaller, 'family' firms. Growth in their size and the scope of their business has not, in general, been underpinned by a growth in professionalism in management. Windfall profits, arising from high interest rates and exchange rate movements favourable to their business, have tended to cover the lack of managerial skill and experience. The rate of growth, current size of organisations and nature of the markets are tending to lead to an increasing awareness of the need for greater professionalism in the management of their business.

This realisation of the need for change in the broking world was summed up by Derek Day (Managing Director, Alexander Howden Management and Data Services Ltd):

Change is coming in the broking world. There is an increasing realisation that there is a need for improved professionalism. The sector has grown beyond the level which can be supported by existing skilled and matured talent. There is a high degree of technical maturity, but a lack of managerial skill and maturity.

The underwriting cycles on the commercial business side affect the large, national brokers since, in a 'soft' market, the premiums on which their commission earnings are based decline. This leads to growth plateaux in their business.

The large, national brokers will not be significantly affected by the impending financial services legislation. Their costs may increase in order to deal with legislative registration and inspection requirements. To offset this their market share may grow somewhat as smaller brokers withdraw from the market.

They will clearly face a degree of increased competition from banks and building societies expanding their intermediary activities, and from insurers opting for direct sales marketing strategies. These changes will, however, focus on the personal lines business.

On the commercial side, the main challenges will be related to effective management of their business and making the most of opportunities for growth offered by the upturn in the underwriting cycle.

Summary of issues and trends

Having painted a broad picture of the changes taking place in the main component parts of the financial sector, it is useful to draw together the common issues faced by organisations.

In terms of formulating management development strategy and policies, it is important that these issues and their implications are clearly understood. If management development is to become more than a peripheral activity it must make a real, and significant, contribution to the resolution of the major issues being faced and to the survival and growth of the business.

The major common issues to be faced would seem to be:

Continuing change

It is clear that the rate of change in markets, and the general operating environment. will continue to grow. This leads to a need to be able to manage and operate in a volatile and ambiguous climate. Traditional approaches to business planning will no longer hold good in such an environment. The difficulty in identification of future strategies and plans was an issue raised by many of those interviewed.

John Skae (General Manager, Group Resources, Legal and General Group) viewed the situation as follows:

The current rate of change and levels of uncertainty in the financial sector means that it is impossible to know what will happen in the medium to long term.

John Horner (Corporate Planning Manager, Lombard Continental) said that:

> In practice it has become very difficult to go beyond a three year period for corporate planning purposes.

The problems in corporate planning come through clearly into the formulation of management development strategy. David Woodward (Group Personnel Director of Scandinavian Bank) identified uncertainty as a major problem:

> Around five years ago you could reckon on being able to predict the skills that would be required in five years' time. In the current climate it is no longer possible to do this.

The challenge for an organisation in such a climate is to develop a strategy for managing such a rate of change and taking advantage of the opportunities offered by less regulated and more open markets.

Products

In most areas in the sector there are fundamental changes taking place in terms of the range, nature and complexity of products. The view that 'money is a homogeneous product' is leading to an elimination of traditional segmentation. No longer will an organisation be able to look to a secure traditional product base which is unlikely to be challenged by new competitors.

All organisations will face the need to manage an expanded product range, extending well beyond their core business experience and expertise. Not only will ranges be expanded, but products will also have shorter life cycles. The homogeneity of the market will result in smaller 'windows' in which individual organisations can take advantage of competitive advantage arising from product differentiation.

There appears an increasing need for flexibility in product design to ensure customer needs and expectations are satisfied.

Marketing focus

The reduced product differentiation is giving rise to an increasing emphasis on the development and maintenance of customer relationships.

As information on products and services proliferates, customers are becoming increasingly sophisticated and demanding. The organisations that will survive and flourish are those that get close to their customers. The pressure to do this will grow as the number of competitors in the market increases.

In the corporate markets, the institutional investors will gain even greater influence. Their views will need to be listened to, and responded to, in terms of product, service and value for money. The customer focus will need to be sharpened considerably. The management of customer relationships will acquire a higher profile in successful organisations. For example, continuity in customer relationships may assume a level of importance which acts as a barrier to moving key people into new or alternative jobs.

On the retail side of the business, the customer focus will be reflected in the nature and layout of retail branches and outlets. As important will be changes in the way these outlets are managed and the skill which will be required by branch staff.

Whether in corporate or retail markets, a real challenge will be that of communication. As the reduction of product differentiation grows the challenge will be considerable. In the words of Malcolm Parker of Citicorp Investment Bank:

> As a result of competition we have to ensure that we effectively communicate with our customers. The benefits of doing business with us have to be clearly spelled out to customers in bottom line terms.

Organisation

To deal with the changes in markets and products there is need to look at the way in which businesses are organised.

At the corporate end of the market, diverse companies have merged in the lead up to, and wake of, 'Big Bang'. To succeed, these businesses must effectively integrate the diverse organisations, produce a new structure designed to capitalise on the opportunities presented and effectively respond to customer demands.

Expansion of product ranges in the retail markets is leading to a need for importation of new skills. As at the corporate level, there is a need for organisations to be modified to enable these new skills to be effectively integrated so that they may add value rather than create problems.

Given the rate of change in the markets, and the continuing dramatic impact of information technology, companies will need to have a far more flexible view of their approach to organisation. The period of stable organisation structures being seen as a mark of effective management has probably passed. Success may well be associated with the ability to view organisation structures as transient, being related to specific business goals and market needs.

Successful organisations will need to combine the ability to effectively integrate diverse skills, and provide central direction and guidance, with the flexibility necessary to enable them to be opportunistic and take advantage of favourable market opportunities or 'windows'.

Efficiency

Customers, be they corporate or retail, have clearly benefited from the changes which have been taking place in the financial sector.

The move to a more flexible, customer-oriented, approach to business requires that organisations are more efficient in developing, delivering and supporting their services. Quality and efficiency of service are likely to become features which differentiate organisations in the customers' eyes.

At the same time increased competition has placed pressure on traditional margins. This will force organisations to seek to improve efficiency in order to maintain profitability. The growing trend to fee-related income, and reduction in interest-based income, will again sharpen the awareness of the need for real efficiency and the need to project and communicate this efficiency to the customer.

People

Organisations are faced with a need to acquire or develop new skills and talents in their people. Along with competition for business has come fierce competition for people with the skills and talents deemed necessary to develop new products and services. This has resulted in an escalation of salaries for those with skills in high demand. Given the rate of change in markets and products, and the need to develop people with skills to manage the businesses, these premia on specific skills may act as a barrier for some organisations. They may either inhibit entry to a particular market or act as a barrier to the development of broader based managerial skills, as people will be drawn to the development of skills offering such high levels of reward.

A major issue facing many organisations in the sector is that relating to strategies for acquiring and retaining people with the skills needed to achieve business goals.

To succeed it is necessary to develop policies which will ensure that, once skilled people are in position, they are retained and grown to meet the future needs of the business. The penalties of getting it wrong are significant. If a business fails to effectively develop and reward its people, the level of competition will ensure that they are acquired by a business with more effective policies.

It has been recognised, by a number of organisations, that the successful businesses are good at protecting their best people from being poached. They are also good at spotting and developing talent.

The focus is also shifting from individuals to teams. Increasingly teams are moving from one organisation to another. The need for integration of diverse skills, to effectively compete in the market, is accompanied by a realisation of the need to look at developing and rewarding teams of people as well as individuals.

Overall it is recognised that people decisions have moved to the cutting edge of a business. In a sector which has always publicly stated that its people are its most important asset there is now a realisation that, unless people decisions are right, there is a real possibility of failure in a business sense.

These issues and trends present significant challenges to businesses in the financial sector. Most of the major issues have a strong people dimension and call for effective management of the business. This presents an exciting opportunity for those concerned with management development. The opportunity exists for management development to be firmly established as a significant element in the overall strategy for the survival and growth of a business.

Robin Leigh Pemberton (Governor of the Bank of England), in commenting on the issues of deregulation and changes in the market, said:

Change is exhilarating, but also uncomfortable. The prize is a stronger and more vigorous financial services industry.

This sentiment applies to most of the businesses within the sector. The 'prize' for those who effectively manage the change is a stronger and more vigorous business. The focus of management development strategy in these organisations must be on contributing to the resolution of the major issues and the surmounting of the barriers which need to be overcome to succeed in this stimulating environment.

2 The Role of Tomorrow's Manager

The preceding chapter has painted a picture of a volatile and uncertain environment in the financial sector. This tends to beg the question – What type of managers will be needed to enable a business to succeed in such an environment?

Perhaps to answer this question we need to consider other questions, including:

● What will be the structure of future management jobs, and the demands on managers, in the future?
● What skills will be required to effectively fulfil such jobs?
● In what type of organisational structure will the future managers' job be set?
● Will all managers require the same range and mix of skills?

Before a successful management development strategy can be formulated it is necessary to have answers to these questions. It is important that, as with any strategic planning, there is a model embodying the assumptions about the future and which provides a framework for deciding on actions to be taken.

In the field of developing managers a number of generic models exist. Many of these are built upon the assumptions that there exists a body of 'generalisable' managerial skills applicable to most organisations.

In their book *Tomorrow's Men Today*, Andrew and Valerie Stewart presented the results of their research into the factors and characteristics relating to effective managers. They found that only around a third of the factors and characteristics identified applied across a range of different managerial jobs. They did produce a profile of 9 core characteristics of successful managers. These characteristics were:

– Self-management
– Individual decision-making
– Group decision-making
– Relations with peers and superiors
– Management of subordinates

- Attitudes to change
- Social skills
- Communication
- Specialist skills and knowledge

It certainly would be possible to take these core characteristics as a basis for training and education geared to providing effective managers. There is certainly no reason to believe that these characteristics, and their correlation with effective management, do not hold good in the financial sector. However, in relation to the questions posed at the start of this chapter, there appears to be a need for a more detailed model to cover the dynamics of development to meet the needs of the future.

Another study, carried out in the UK by Professor Margerison (*How Chief Executives Succeed*), examined the requirements for success as a top manager. This study involved interviewing senior executives and obtaining responses from a larger group by means of a questionnaire. One part of this study looked at senior managements' perceptions of the things which were important in helping them to achieve success.

In this part of the study there were five factors which were overwhelmingly endorsed as being of great importance. These were:

- The ability to work with a wide variety of different people in different situations
- A need to achieve results
- Early overall responsibility for important tasks rather than trivial delegation
- Early experience of leadership
- Wide experience of many managerial functions before the age of 35

In the same way that the Stewart's characteristics could form an agenda for management training and education, Margerison's findings could be seen as providing a framework for a broader approach to management development.

While both of these sets of findings clearly go some way to providing a framework on which to build a management development strategy, in order to answer our earlier questions there is a need to look further. The degree of change being faced by organisations in the financial sector makes it increasingly difficult to develop a clear view of the future nature of managerial jobs, and a detailed profile of the skills required. Yet, as a starting point for formulating a management development strategy, it is necessary to make some assumptions about both the nature of the jobs and their associated skills.

In building management development programmes it appears that, in relation to a view on future managerial requirements, three main options are available. These are:

● To assume that the basic structure of managerial jobs will remain much the same as at present.

● To look at the way in which the business appears to be developing and estimate the future shape and structure of managerial jobs.

● To assume that the rate of change and degree of uncertainty in the markets will continue. Based on this assumption, the skills that will enable managers to cope in such an environment are identified. Strategy then focuses on fostering and developing these skills rather than on developing skills related to clearly defined future jobs.

In order to develop a clear picture of the talents and skills required by future managers, it is necessary to have a view of the overall shape and structure of the organisation. The rate of extension of product ranges, and changes in product life cycle and mix, raises questions about the future shape of organisations in the financial sector. Currently many organisations are structured on a centralised, single business basis. In such structures there are functional or product-based divisions. However, there tends to be a basic assumption that managerial roles are essentially common and that skills are transferrable between many divisions. These assumptions underpin the organisation's approach to management development. The clearing banks and building societies frequently tend to be structured on this basis.

The increasing diversity of products and markets, coming within the scope of single businesses in the sector, is leading to alternative views on organisation emerging. The two main alternatives are:

1. Separate business unit organisation

This approach to structuring the business is based upon identifying different product areas or market segments as being different business units. Each unit is seen to have differing needs in terms of management style, marketing, structure, skills and talents. For example, the style and structure of the retail banking unit of a 'composite bank' would be very different to that of the investment banking unit.

In such a structure the separate business units tend to operate with a high degree of autonomy. The corporate role tends to be one of establishing broad guidelines, in terms of performance requirements, and corporate strategic direction. This approach to organisation is managed either on a holding company basis (for example, the structure adopted by the Legal and General Assurance Group) or on a divisionalised basis (a structure used by the Scandinavian Bank).

From a management development viewpoint, the 'legal' structure is not the significant issue. What is important is the recognition that different business units have differing needs in terms of managerial style, skills and experience. In addition there is a recognition that group or corporate management has yet again differing needs in terms of managerial style and skills.

The distinct advantages of such an approach to organisation are that it becomes relatively easy to respond to differing market needs and to change emphasis on products or market segments as the environment changes (including establishing new units to enter new markets).

2. Matrix organisations

Particularly noticeable in the commercial and investment banking areas is an increasing tendency to move to a matrix-based organisation structure.

This tendency is being driven by the need for effective integration in order to successfully compete in this sector of the market.

To a large extent, this approach to organisation recognises that different parts of the business have needs for different skills and styles or working. To meet the demands of the market it is recognised that these skills need to be brought together. However, the problems of trying to encompass the diverse styles and skills in a unitary structure are recognised, and transient relationships are established to meet a shared business need. The major problems encountered in matrix-based organisations appear to relate to the

complexity of managing a wider range of relationship and difficulty
in pinpointing accountability for many areas of management.

The way in which the organisation is structured has a major
impact on the approach to formulating management development
strategy. The differing structures have a major influence on views on
the future structure of management jobs.

In talking to senior management in a range of financial sector
organisations, there seemed to be three major views on the emerging
structure and nature of future management jobs. These were:

Steady state

Although recognising the fundamental changes taking place in the
market, a number of organisations held the view that the basic
nature and structure of managerial jobs (particularly senior
management jobs) would not change. This view was developed from
a picture of the structure of the organisation as a centralised unified
business. The extended range of products was seen as creating a
need for new specialists. Such extensions were perceived as doing
little more than extending the range of services to be managed by
senior level managers.

In organisations with this view of the future structure it was
recognised that managers will require further skills to respond
effectively to market changes. However, the basic structure of the
jobs and organisations would not change.

Management development planning in such organisations is largely
based upon a model of equipping managers to provide continuity in
succession into jobs structured on the same basis as at present. The
main thrust of development is on replicating past development
patterns and extending the range of skills to meet new conditions.

Core skills

Organisations who viewed their future structure as continuing on a
unified basis did not all have the 'steady state' view on the future
structure of managerial jobs within the organisation. In these
organisations there is a recognition that, as the nature of the market
changes, so will the structure of the management jobs. The rate of
change in the sector is seen as being such that it is difficult to predict
the future structure of jobs. However, given the 'unified' organisation

structure, it is felt that managers will be able to adapt to changes if core skills are effectively developed. In these organisations management development strategy is geared to the identification of future core skills and the identification of people either possessing these skills or capable of acquiring them.

Business managers

The view that, in the future, a financial sector organisation will be made up of a disparate range of separate business units is becoming increasingly prevalent, as companies extend and diversify their range of products and services. Organisations taking this view see that managerial jobs, and associated skills, will vary significantly from business unit to business unit. This view of organisation, and the future structure of jobs, is found in companies operating on a holding company basis with business units being subsidiaries in a group, and in single company structures where the separate business unit is housed in a division rather than a subsidiary company.

The separate business-unit philosophy allows for greater scope in achieving a match between individual skills and job requirements. It also allows for greater flexibility in allowing individual business units to respond differently to the needs of the market segment in which they operate. Because the separate units operate on a fairly autonomous basis, changes in strategy, structure and methods of operating can be made relatively quickly, without having to be integrated into the overall business structure.

This approach to organisation enables differing units to develop managers to fulfil specific requirements and acquire specific skills related closely to their business needs. It is a particularly valuable structure, given the volatility of the market and the tendency to shorten product life cycles.

For example, in a banking organisation the investment banking business unit may be in a high growth area. The managers in this unit would need to be highly entrepreneurial and have excellent marketing skills. There would also be a need for a high degree of product innovation and good technical knowledge relating to the operation of the market and product structures. The traditional wholesale banking unit of the same organisation may well be at a mature stage of its business cycle. Managers in this unit would be likely to be focusing on optimising the returns available. Their job would be more focused on control of costs, and people management geared to improving productivity in a zero or low growth environment.

Within the same bank there may also be business units which are concerned with a declining part of the market. For example, an overseas bank in London may see its retail business as a market from which it wishes to withdraw. Managers in this unit would be concerned with effectively managing the closure or divestment of all or part of the operation. This would result in a job structured differently, and requiring different skills, from both those in the growing and mature parts of the overall business.

The Legal and General provide a good example of an insurance company which has opted for the separate business unit structure. In fact they are organised on a group holding company basis with subsidiary operating companies in each of the major market areas. Top management in each subsidiary is assessed in the light of the results achieved. As long as performance is at desired level, the management are allowed a high degree of freedom in operational matters. The Royal Insurance Group have also moved to a similarly organisational structure.

Allied Dunbar (formerly Hambro Life) have a strong commitment to the decentralisation of business management. However, in their case the focus of the division into business units is their branch network. As the range of their products extends into the financial services business, branch managers are seen as business managers, with an evolving accountability for the overall performance and profitability of their branches. Within general guidelines, business objectives and an overall company philosophy, they enjoy considerable autonomy in the way in which they run their business unit.

In the banking area, Scandinavian Bank have recognised that different business areas require different skills and approaches to management. They too provide an example of movement to a separate business unit philosophy. Indeed they are also looking at areas providing support services (for example, personnel, data processing) as potentially being run as business units, with their market being both internal and external.

Adoption of a separate business unit philosophy and structure carries with it a need to recognise that the nature and structure of jobs throughout the organisation will vary considerably. This makes for difficulty in central planning of management development. The difficulty is overcome, in part, in organisations such as Legal and

General, by decentralising accountability for operational management development to the operating units. In this way much management development planning is carried out by those closer to the market place, having a clearer view of the units' business needs. Consequently a clearer picture may be built of the likely future structure of management jobs.

In such organisations there remains a need for group or corporate management. Movement to a separate business unit philosophy in itself changes the shape and structure of corporate management jobs. One of the key corporate challenges is to balance the need to allow operational units freedom of action with the need to ensure the continuity of skilled managers available to fill corporate roles.

In order to achieve this balance it is common to find that corporate management development is a central responsibility. To meet corporate needs the senior management of operating units may be directed and subjected to constraints on their own development plans for specific individuals.

In the financial sector, whichever organisational philosophy is adopted, there is a recognition that the nature of managerial jobs is, and will continue to be, changing. The degree to which the change is perceived, and its consequent impact on management development strategy, is certainly least in those organisations with a 'steady state' view of structure and organisational development.

Clearly it is not possible in a book such as this to provide a detailed picture of people's views of future job structures. However, it is possible to summarise perceptions of the main changes in the nature of management jobs in the sector.

Increasing market focus

In the majority of organisations in the sector there is a recognition that many meaningful jobs will need to be increasingly outward looking. Managers' actions will need to be more geared to what is happening in the market, or segment of the market in which they are operating. They will need to ensure that their areas respond rapidly, and effectively, to market changes and needs in order that the business retains, or gains, a competitive edge wherever possible.

Many organisations in the sector expressed the view that currently the complexities of the business are so great that, to survive and grow, it is critical to have a cutting edge and to be sharp in the competitive areas.

Resource management

Managers' jobs will broaden, from the commonly-perceived base of being a skilled and experienced technician, to that of a manager of resources. Managers will be increasingly expected to contribute to the business planning process, and to identify the full range of resources needed to achieve agreed goals and objectives. Performance will be increasingly evaluated on the basis of how effectively financial, human and technological resources have been employed, rather than on a task completion basis.

Greater freedom and discretion

There appears to be a wide recognition that decisions need to be taken 'near to the seat of the action'. The financial sector has traditionally operated on a highly-centralised decision-making basis. Managers' jobs have been surrounded by precedents, guidelines, procedural rules and other contraints on action. This limiting of freedom of decision-making is not conducive to the rapid responses, and initiation of action, required in a competitive and volatile market.

There is a move towards establishing clear objectives for managers and allowing greater freedom in action in achieving these objectives. The 'price' of such freedom is a much more sharply focused approach to performance evaluation.

This devolution of authority is likely to pass down through the managerial strata. In particular this is likely to impact on the nature of middle management jobs. The conversion of ideas and strategy into action rests on the organisation's middle managers. Providing them with greater freedom and discretion will provide an earlier experience of the decision-making process used at general management level. It is the middle managers who will, hopefully, provide the future general managers.

Overall, managers' decisions will be driven more by the requirements of the job and business than by organisational procedures and constraints. Peter Rowe (Chief Manager, Training Co-ordination, Lloyds Bank) summarises this change nicely:

In the future, at most levels in the organisation, commercial awareness and business needs will drive the management of human, financial and technical resources.

Increasing relationship management

The rapid extension of product ranges, levels of innovation and introduction of new products and services will make it increasingly difficult for managers to have in-depth technical knowledge relating to all of the areas under their control.

At the same time, in many organisations, rigid reporting lines and structures will be replaced by either transient or matrix structures. To effectively operate in such an environment, greater emphasis will be placed on managers' responsibility for effectively managing relationships. This will apply particularly to the need for effective management of professionals and specialists outside of the managers' own specialism. It will also apply to the need to work in matrix or transient structures securing results through persuasion and influence rather than through position power and authority.

The challenge facing many organisations will be that of broadening 'hands on' specialists to be able to fulfill such a different role.

Focus on team working

An increased need to manage specialists and professionals will call for a team-based management style.

At the same time the need for an organisation to be able to retain competitive positions will give rise to a need for flexible and rapid responses to market changes.

To be able to do this will require effective integration of a diverse range of functions increasing responsiveness to customer and market demands. This gives rise to an increasing need for managers to be able to work on a team basis with colleagues.

The pressure for team working will impact on all levels of an organisation as the business becomes more complex. Dr Guth, of Deutsche Bank, clearly identified this requirement:

According to my experience, there is no area in banking where efficient teamwork does not produce quicker and better results that the greatest of efforts by talented individuals alone. Certainly when it comes to selling our products, very much depends on the ability of the individual to convince the customer. But even the 'star' salesmen need a backroom team to handle quickly and efficiently the business they bring home. This is where teamwork comes into play. The same need for teamwork applies without reservation to the top executive body, the board of directors.

Greater involvement in planning and strategic management

Along with greater freedom and discretion, and an increased market focus, goes a delegation of responsibility for business planning. Traditionally, in the financial sector, managers have worked to achieve results directed by a top level driven business plan.

Increasingly diversity within markets is giving rise to a need to decentralise planning and obtain input to corporate plans from the 'seat of the action'. Involvement of managers in corporate business planning is increasing the need for them to consider strategic issues as they apply to their product, business unit or market segment.

This represents, for many, a significant change in the nature of their job. Derek Day (Managing Director of Alexander Howden Management and Data Services Limited) sees this as a major issue in both insurance broking and the sector overall:

In insurance broking, and indeed the whole of the financial sector, too many senior managers are only geared up to working within the parameters of an established business plan. Not enough have had the experience of or exposure to the practice of strategic management which is becoming an increasingly significant aspect of their job.

Dennis Brockwell (Assistant General Manager, Field Operations, Nationwide Building Society) sees business and strategic planning as already falling within the remit of regional managers. He envisages these elements figuring in the jobs of branch managers in the not too distant future.

The above areas of change, represent, for many organisations, a move to a significantly different structure and shape of managerial jobs. The process of management development needs to be built around this view of these jobs. The rate of change in the sector has, as already identified, made it difficult to predict the future profile of management jobs. However, the fact that change is already taking place is clear. Crawford Laughlan, of the Halifax Building Society, comments on his experience, which is representative of that of many others:

In our branches the key questions are what skills will we need and what products will we be selling? It is clear that new skills will be needed in the branches if we are to provide a full range of financial services.

New skill requirements are already emerging in the Head Office setting. For example, in the investment area we now require new skills due to the growth in wholesale funding activities.

A clear picture of the major changes identified here will help to provide some direction for future management development planning.

In both the Royal Group and the Legal and General the need to develop specific future job profiles as a core to management development planning is recognised. The Legal and General have, for top level jobs, moved towards implementing a programme of identifying future key criteria, in terms of specific skills and behaviour.

At the Royal the question as to who should be responsible for developing profiles has been seriously considered. The Group is now divided into a number of operating companies, each of whom is responsible for its own personnel work. The Group, however, does retain accountability for ensuring that there is a satisfactory succession situation and for appointing managers to the top 30 or so posts in the Group worldwide. The balance between decentralisation and ensuring common standards is being achieved through agreement about broad profiles for top, middle and junior management, which have been so defined that they represent approximately similar positions throughout the organisation.

There has, however, been a need to ensure that, as jobs have been changing so fast, their profile is not just today's job but the one that is required in the future. To this end a comprehensive strategy statement has been prepared in respect of personnel matters which effectively describes the culture that is being sought. The role profiles are related directly to this. Scandinavian Bank found that, when following this route, current managers based their profiles on their own past experience, rather than a broader view of the future of the bank, its business and its markets.

Success at the Legal and General has come from discussion and examination of skills and characteristics required by managers rather than a tight definition of the job.

Although in many organisations it is difficult to develop a clear

picture of the future nature of management jobs, there appears to
be a fairly good view of the skills and abilities which will be required
to succeed in the volatile and changing markets. The main skills and
abilities identified were remarkably common in all types of
organisation in the financial sector. The following synopsis highlights
the main common skills and abilities identified as being required by
a future manager in the financial sector.

Flexibility and adaptability

Amongst both senior management and training and development
specialists in all types of organisation, there was complete agreement
that, both now and in the future, managers will need to be highly
flexible and adaptable. The changing and volatile nature of the
markets leads to changes in demands on managers and business
priorities. Not only is it difficult to clearly identify the nature of
future jobs, it is becoming increasingly necessary to adapt current
jobs to meet changing market needs. Managing within clear
guidelines, policies and operating precedents is, in many parts of
businesses, becoming increasingly difficult. The nature of the sector
is such that it is difficult for top management to provide stable, long-
term directions and tactical plans.

Such an environment requires managers who are capable of
coping with ambiguity and changes in demands and priorities.

Commercial awareness

The financial sector is rapidly moving to a customer focus in its
marketing and product development. Most managers will be required
to be more responsive to the needs of, and changes in, the market
segment in which they are operating. This gives rise to the need for
managers to have a much broader view of their role. The need will
be for managers who are able to see their job, and contribution, in a
wider context. They will need to be able to relate to their
organisation, and an area within that organisation, as a business in a
commercial market. More decisions will need to be evaluated in a
commercial context.

In some organisations there is a view that managers must
increasingly have entrepreneurial skills. In my view most financial
sector organisations neither need, nor could cope with, a large influx
of entrepreneurs. These skills may be needed in the new product

areas and fast-growing business units. However, I feel, that in many cases, what is termed a need for entrepreneurial skills is, in fact, a need for the ability to manage with a greater awareness of the commercial environment in which the job is operating.

In some ways this 'skill' area may be expressed as managers needing 'helicopter' vision. At the Abbey National, Peter Birch sees it as vital that managers at all levels develop this broader perspective, saying:

> It is essential to develop 'helicopter vision' in all managers. They need to be able to rise above the confines of their specialisms.

In referring to 'confines of specialisms', Peter Birch usefully identifies one way of looking at commercial awareness. Traditionally, many managers have been developed to be inwardly focused on a specialist area of activity. The process of promotion has often been based upon evidence of technical excellence. The need now is for a fundamental change to an external focus, and a need to operate in a way which meets market and business demands.

Ability to learn

The rate of change, in both markets and technology, is resulting in managers having to learn to undertake new tasks, cope with changed priorities, and to operate in new ways.

This is giving rise to a need to find and develop managers with an ability to learn quickly. The expected continuation of a high rate of change will make it difficult to mount regular, centrally-directed, training initiatives. Managers will need to have the ability to initiate and manage their own learning if they are to keep pace with the change and operate effectively.

In many organisations this is seen as a key skill area. At Lloyds Bank, Peter Rowe sees the need for a major emphasis in their management development programmes to be on helping managers to understand the learning process. In an uncertain and volatile environment he sees this as being a very important element in future management skills training.

Intellectual dexterity

As business becomes more complex and less subject to clear

guidelines and precedents, a need arises for managers to possess 'intellectual dexterity'.

It is difficult to clearly define what is meant by 'intellectual dexterity'. What does seem clear is that managers will have to have the intellect, experience and background to really think through issues. Decisions will have to encompass a greater number of variables, and have potentially a wider range of implications, than has been the case in the past.

The nature of decision-making will broaden. The number of decisions based upon hard, quantitative data within clearly defined parameters will be greatly reduced. Increasingly, the need for prompt reaction to market requirements, in a complex business, will need managers capable of making qualitative decisions. In many ways 'intellectual dexterity' may be seen as the ability to read situations and use available information together with an understanding of the nature of the business, to make qualitative decisions.

Decisiveness

Greater decentralisation of the decision-making process combined with a need for qualitative decisions will lead to a need for managers to be able to be decisive. Action will need to be taken quickly, which reduces the facility to 'second guess' decisions, or submit them to an approval or sanctioning process.

This will give rise to a need for courage in decision-making and resilience on the part of managers. Managers will need to be tough. They will have to be able to take knocks and still be positive and commercially sensitive in their decision-making.

As businesses move into dealing with an increasing range of products, managers will, to a large extent, be more isolated and independent. They will need to have the sensitivity to be able to read the environment and take decisions based on their judgement.

Communication skills

Increasing complexity, uncertainty and volatility in the environment will place a premium on a wide range of communication skills.

The ability to effectively communicate externally with customers, shareholders and other stakeholders is seen as vital in contributing to survival and growth. At the same time, internal communication of business goals, values and strategies is seen as being increasingly important in offsetting the potential problems of operating in uncertain and rapidly changing environments.

Jack Rutley (Management Development Manager of the Nationwide Building Society) has found that, in discussing development needs with his Assistant General Managers, they all perceive their most pressing need as being the acquisition of improved communication skills. In the Nationwide it is clearly perceived that the route through to general management is dependent upon the possession of a high level of communication skills.

Internally, organisations will increasingly move away from operating on the basis of authority derived from position. The complexity of the business will require a much greater emphasis on cross-functional decision-making. This places a premium on effective management of relationships, with decisions reached upon the basis of persuasion and effective communication of the need for, and nature of, actions to be taken.

Growing segregation of business units gives rise to a need for effective communication of corporate strategy and values together with flows of information on the activities and achievements of the individual units. Without such effective corporate communication the business could fragment to a degree which would make it extremely difficult to manage from an overall view point.

Thus communication skills are becoming increasingly vital at all levels of management within organisations.

Marketing and selling skills

Although selling skills may be seen as a specific form of communication skill, the fundamental shift of the sector to a customer focus warrants their separate mention.

More managerial jobs will entail interaction with customers. Survival and growth will depend on managers being able to sell to their customers. Selling skills, in this sense, relate to the ability to effectively understand and ascertain customers' needs, and to present solutions in a way which clearly shows bottom line benefits to the customer. As competitive product differentiation becomes more difficult to achieve, greater emphasis will be placed on developing good customer relationships. Organisations will need to position themselves to meet a wide range of needs. These two requirements mean that managers will not only be selling their own 'products' but will also need to cross-sell 'products' available elsewhere in the organisation.

An increasing commercial and market focus requires managers to possess the skills and abilities to read what is happening in their immediate market place. Not only is the skill that of 'reading' the market, but also being able to respond in terms of developing products and services to meet the needs of the market. In this sense, managers will require marketing as well as selling skills.

Whilst most of the above comments will appear readily applicable to managers with customer, product or service responsibilities, their relevance to other areas of management may be more obscure. However, if managers throughout the organisation are to be more commercially aware, and less dependent upon position power to achieve results, then marketing and selling skills are also important.

For the technical specialist there will be a need to become involved in supporting the marketing and selling effort. Success in non-line functions (for example, personnel) will become dependent upon successful marketing and selling of services within the organisation.

Ability to take a broad view

This skill has, in part, been highlighted in referring to a need for commercial awareness. However, it is worth mentioning separately as it comes into play in a number of contexts.

The manager of the future will be dealing with an increasingly complex range of products or services. To effectively operate there will be a need to manage groups of specialists and professionals. This in turn will require a much broader understanding of an increasingly wide range of activities. Managers will have to exhibit a broad understanding, without having the expertise and technical depth which has traditionally characterised the structure of management jobs in the financial sector.

The other element of breadth of vision is more externally directed. Managers will need to be able to take a broad based, and well-informed, view of the market-place. John Horner (Corporate Planning Manager, Lombard Continental) identifies this element of breadth clearly:

Managers will need the breadth of vision to spot opportunities to take and (importantly) those *not* to take.

The need for breadth in banking was highlighted in Dr Guth's paper to the International Conference on Bank Training in 1986.

> Let me make a few remarks on the subject of knowledge and experience in banking. They should, of course, be as broad as possible. This applies above all to those whose talents and inner drive mark them out as potential managers. Specialists without broad banking background have only limited value, because in the banking business everything is somehow interrelated.

Interpersonal skills

For a long time now much of the emphasis in management training has focused on the development and improvement of interpersonal skills.

In the financial sector people are one of the major resources. Thus it is inevitable that, as business pressures push for improved performance, managers will need to improve their abilities in managing one of the major resources.

The changes in organisation structure and style, with reduced dependence on rules and position power, increased use of specialists and emphasis on relationship management both internally and externally, increase the need for managers to possess high level interpersonal skills.

Technical skills

The 'traditional' route to management in the financial sector has been through technical excellence. There is a great danger that, in reviewing the managers' role and skills in the current climate of change, the importance of technical competence and excellence could be lost sight of.

Increasingly customers are seeking high levels of professionalism and competence in the financial sector. Future managers will require technical competence in their own sphere of specialism as a foundation on which other skills are to be built.

However, the balance between technical competence and the other skills identified is important. Technical competence must be seen in relation to the demands of the job rather than a goal in its own right.

Garrett Bouton on Scandinavian Bank summarises the balance in his bank, as follows:

Managers need to be technically competent, but only to the degree necessary to do their jobs. There are going to be times when management and leadership qualities are more important than technical competence. Managers must be able to motivate others and achieve results through the competence of others.

The above summary is by no means exhaustive. It represents a common view in the financial sector of the key skills required by managers in the future. In addition there appears a high degree of consensus that managers will also require the following skills and abilities:

- Numeracy
- Technological awareness and interest
- Planning skills
- Analytical ability

Overall it represents a formidable list to which the key characteristic of stamina should be added!

SUMMARY

In many financial sector organisations there is a view that management development strategy must be based upon a clear understanding of the nature, structure and demands of future jobs rather than on an assumption of a continuation of current structures. However, given the rate of change, and degree of uncertainty, in the sector it is difficult to be clear as to the precise shape of future jobs. What does appear clear is that the nature of the jobs are changing and that the main changes are:

- Increasing market focus
- Greater freedom of action and discretion
- Increasing degree of relationship management
- Focus on team working
- Greater involvement in planning and strategic management

Effective performance of managerial jobs will require new skills and a changed emphasis on existing ones. The common view of the core future skills and abilities of managers is that they will require to be:

- Flexible and adaptable
- Commercially aware
- Able to learn rapidly
- Intellectually dexterous
- Decisive
- Effective communicators
- Marketeers and salespeople
- Able to take a broad view
- Effective in interpersonal relationships
- Technically competent

There will, however, be no universal profile. Increasingly the structure of jobs and balance of skills will be matched to the environment in which the manager's business unit is operating, and the stage of products and services in their life cycle.

The profile emerging does not give a common agenda for management training. It does, however, point to some imperatives for the formulation of management development strategy. These relate to the need to develop profiles for both jobs and individuals in order that the most effective match may be achieved.

Increasingly, in the sector, interest will be focused on management development strategies geared to the identification and development of skills and abilities geared to providing people capable of fulfilling the current, and future, business needs of the organisation.

J. M. Harries, writing in *Training and Development* ('Should Management Development be a Three Way Contract?' – July 1986), commented broadly on the future strategy for training and development in the UK. His words are very relevant to the needs of the financial sector:

In any crystal ball exercise concerned with training and development practice in the United Kingdom, we would argue that the fundamental plank on which strategy might be built must be the development of managers to enable them to cope more effectively with conditions likely to obtain in the foreseeable future. Any other approach is, as best, tangential.

He argues that concentration on specific topics or techniques is not fundamentally effective and concludes:

it is only through the process of improving the fundamental qualities of British managers that this country can be equipped to survive and flourish in the next ten years and beyond.

3 A Shift in Focus

The first two chapters have illustrated that the financial sector is facing fundamental and far-reaching change. This change will require major changes in the nature of management jobs and a new perception of the skills and abilities required to perform these jobs effectively.

In this chapter the implications of these changes, in terms of how management development is perceived in the sector, are examined. If management development is to play a significant role in contributing to helping organisations cope with fundamental change it is important to establish a clear view of the factors which are the key to a development programme's success. This chapter also examines views, within the sector, on the critical success factors which must apply to a management development programme.

The basic questions examined, then, are:

● How are perceptions of the nature, and scope, of management development changing?

● What are the critical success factors for a future management development strategy?

● How is the success of a management development programme to be judged?

● What are the key ingredients, or components, of an effective management development programme?

● How can these critical success factors be built into management development strategies and programmes?

The perceptions of management development in the financial sector have, to a large extent, been influenced by the relatively comfortable environment in which organisations have operated. The traditional perception was summarised rather nicely by David Salmon, Secretary (Education and Training) of the Chartered Insurance Institute:

In the past many insurance organisations have been highly centralised in terms of decision-making, with little real delegation

45

of responsibility. Rigid frameworks and rule systems have been developed with the aim of preventing mistakes and errors.

This situation has also prevailed in banks and building societies.

The result has been a comfortable, unresponsive environment, in which the need to invest in and look for returns from management development has not been perceived at a senior level.

As pointed out in earlier chapters, this comfortable environment has changed dramatically. As the environment changes, and the need for managers with new skills emerges, so does the thinking on the importance of people in relation to achieving business goals.

The profile of the 'future manager' outlined in Chapter 2 gives rise to a need for organisations to review their approach to recruiting and developing people. The commonly expressed 'motherhood' that 'people are our most important resource' is becoming recognised as a business reality. The high cost of acquiring people with special skills and talents has demonstrated the financial consequences of failing to place a sufficiently high priority on developing staff.

The changed priority and perception has far-reaching effects in terms of the strategy for developing people. It is recognised that it is insufficient to look at training and education alone. Any effective strategy will have to encompass recruitment, career planning, reward and promotion, as well as training and education.

Melvyn Howell, of the Midland Bank, sees the need for fundamental change throughout the sector:

There needs to be a fundamental change in thinking amongst insurers, bank and other financial sector organisations in terms of their general approach to recruitment, career and management development. There is a pressing need to recruit bright people who can be developed to rise rapidly through the organisation and, in doing so, acquire the necessary breadth of knowledge and understanding to contribute to the future survival and growth of the business.

The realisation that investment in developing people is critical to the future success of financial sector business is rapidly gaining ground. With this realisation there has come a major shift in perceptions of the role and function of management development. Melvyn Howell sees, in his organisation, that:

Management development has shifted from being a concern of the personnel function to being one of general management. It is no longer a 'nice to do' activity or a question of 'good practice'. Management development has become a core business issue.

This shift in perception of management development from an ancillary, personnel-related activity to a central hard business issue is found in many organisations in the sector. It is a view shared by Chief Executives, operational management and personnel specialists. A major indicator of the changed priorities is that increasingly Chief Executives are taking personal responsibility for the issues. For example, Peter Birch, of the Abbey National, is very clear that management development is one of his main areas of accountability. It is an accountability he feels he must effectively fulfil if the Abbey National is going to grow and compete successfully in a tough environment.

Organisations with a track record of high growth and (often) entrepreneurial style are also perceiving a need to look closely at management development. In these organisations the view has been that creating a 'climate for growth' has served them well. Now, however, the issue is becoming so integral to success, in competing in the volatile environment, that a need for a more systematic approach is seen.

Peter Russell, of Allied Dunbar, sees the need to provide for future management needs:

The Company's phenomenal growth record has been achieved by having a highly flexible and innovative organisation. Manpower and succession planning has been on an '*ad hoc*' basis. The challenge now is to improve in these areas and develop a more structured approach, while retaining the responsiveness and flexibility of the organisation. Allied Dunbar has reached the critical mass at which it is necessary to formalise management development systems. In doing so, it is necessary to try to encapture, rather than lose, the benefits of the current flexible, innovative and entrepreneurial style.

Malcolm Parker of Citicorp Investment Bank sees similar issues emerging there:

Citicorp have a good track record in training graduates and

creating a climate which encourages personal growth. However, we have been lacking in the areas of mid-career and senior management training. The chief executive is concerned about this and recognised a need to change. He sees a need to be more structured in the identification and development of high fliers.

Recognition that skilled people can give an organisation a competitive edge has been developing over a number of years. The escalation of salaries, and rapid movement of skilled specialists, has really focused attention on the value of people. The sheer costs involved in recruiting externally to fill key posts has led to a questioning of past views on development. John Horner, of Lombard Continental, sees:

a pressing need to establish effective manpower planning and development. We must move from frequent (and often very expensive) recruitment to meet needs as they arise, to a more systematically planned approach to resourcing the business.

The cost of recruiting staff is one aspect of a wider issue, and that is cost effectiveness. As the market becomes more competitive and the pressure on margins increases, there is a need to examine cost structure. Due to the labour intensive nature of the sector, this process inevitably leads to a need to examine staff costs. In doing this, the dominant concerns are performance and productivity. Are the best returns being achieved from the investment in people?

Viewing people as a significant investment, which can make a major contribution to the success of the business, is a fundamental shift in perception right at the top of many organisations in the sector. Coming with this shift is a realisation that, as with other major investments, a long-term view needs to be taken. The investment needs to be carefully planned and nurtured to realise the optimum returns.

In many organisations, initiatives are being taken at the most senior level to incorporate management development strategy into the overall corporate plan. It is no longer an aspect of management which can be seen as a peripheral or secondary activity.

Derek Day, of Alexander Howden, summarises the changes in perception as he sees them in the insurance market:

Historically, planned training and development has not been seen as an important part of the business plan. However, to have a future it must become an integral part of the day to day business activity . . .

Management within the industry is beginning to understand the need to acquire management skills in order to achieve optimum results. Management are beginning to accept the full responsibilities of being an effective manager, as well as being a professional insurance person. Times are changing. Corporate directors are showing a greater awareness of the need for more professionalism and are putting financial resources behind that commitment.

In a tough market, there is a growing recognition that dependence on enthusiasm, without having developed knowledge and skills, is like running in the dark. Professional training and manpower planning is now perceived as being the key to ensuring that organisations have a successful future.

Overall the changes in views on, and perceptions of, management development may be summarised as:

● Growing recognition of the important role of effective managers in contributing to the achievements of business goals.

● Management development has become a core business issue and shifted from a 'nice to do' personnel activity to a central, general management concern.

● Effective development of people can give an organisation a competitive edge.

● The escalating costs of recruiting specialists has highlighted the danger of relying on external recruitment to fill gaps and meet needs as they arise. A more structured and planned approach is urgently required.

● Competitive pressure on margins has highlighted the need for performance and productivity. People are seen as a long-term investment requiring the same care as other investments.

● Management development strategy is being incorporated into the overall corporate plan.

● Commitment to effective management development often emanates from the Chief Executive.

In many ways it is the growth in top level commitment which is most significant. It is this commitment which reflects the business-driven needs, and which will set new parameters for evaluating the effectiveness of development strategies.

The recognition of the key business role of management developments, and ensuring commitment to it, was highlighted by Jeffrey Hernu (Director of Barclays de Zoette Wedd):

> To succeed in the post 'Big Bang' environment we will need to effectively integrate the new constituent parts of the organisation. This requires effective development of our managers to handle the integration. To succeed in the long term requires ongoing development. To achieve this we need, and indeed have, top down commitment to management development and succession planning.

The changes summarised above reflect changes in views on the importance of, and need for, management development. There are also changes in perception of the scope and nature of management development. Previously in this chapter there have been indications of a broader view of the nature of management development emerging.

It is clear that the outcomes required from management development will not be realised through training and education alone.

Garrett Bouton, of Scandinavian Bank, sees the findings from Margerison's research as clearly indicating the need for a broader view of management development:

> The findings from Margerison's work suggest that management education has an important, but only minor, role in contributing to effective management. Many of the activities and experience which the managers he studied felt were important were those which, in the main, could not be adequately dealt with in the classroom environment. I agree with this view and would suggest that today more than ever there is a need to move people's learning out of the classroom. That is, to set up a better relationship between the education programme and the jobs being done by people. If you like, this could be interpreted as a need to move away from some of the traditional forms of training and move towards planned development.

DEFINITION OF TERMS

Picking up Garrett Bouton's theme, and the needs underpinning the changing views on the importance of management development, it is sensible to look at appropriate definition of terms. ·

Management continuity

It is common to link management succession with management development. However, succession tends to focus on replacement of today's managers. In reality organisations are like societies. They are living things, attempting to endure and grow with one generation succeeding another in changing environments. Thus survival and development implies *continuity*, which provides the ability to effectively operate in the present, and both the vitality and foresight to anticipate and prepare for the future.

Management continuity is broader in scope than management succession. It involves the positioning of the on-going development of managers to perform in changing environments, as well as providing succession for senior posts. Continuity focuses on realising the potential of all managers rather than filling jobs.

In a practical sense, continuity planning requires the development of a sound knowledge of the managerial talent that is currently needed, and available, to meet existing business demands. In addition it requires that future needs be anticipated, and action programmes developed, to ensure that those needs are met.

Management development

In essence, management development is concerned with what an organisation does to ensure that it has the necessary skills and talents available when required, and that necessary performance is effectively delivered.

Management development, when viewed in this way, is far broader than management training and education. It is concerned with focusing on future needs as well as meeting today's needs. The effective operation of development policies involves close links with the processes of assessment and performance evaluation.

Implications

Working within the above definitions implies that management continuity and development will entail involvement with:

● Organisation design
● Recruitment policy and practice
● Job design
● Career planning
● Performance evaluation
● Training and education (general and technical)
● Management training and education
● Manpower planning
● Potential assessment

From this it can be seen that management development strategy is not only an increasingly important issue, but also far broader in scope than has traditionally been seen in many organisations.

Having identified that the perceptions of the role and nature of management developments are changing, it is important to establish the new expectations in terms of what management development should achieve for an organisation.

What is clearly underlying the changed perceptions is that management development strategy is expected to contribute to business performance in a very real sense. Effective management development will be a means of obtaining a competitive edge. It will be a means of an organisation equipping itself to perform better in its markets. Melvyn Howell, of Midland Bank, sees the requirement for management development as follows:

From now on management development must be business driven. Getting it right is vital: getting it wrong is just too expensive. Having a pool of people who can produce the right solutions to business problems, and challenges is now no less important than keeping pace with developments in technology.

This message is strongly reinforced by Donald Kirkham, Chief Executive of the Woolwich Equitable Building Society:

In the current market we can't afford to get the key people decisions wrong. Getting these major decisions right is critical. Failure carries enormously high risks.

The two views represent a fairly general overall expectation relating to the contribution of management development to a business. Exploring expectations in more detail led to the identification of the following common major expectations or requirements:

● *Management development strategy will be business driven*

The view was commonly held that management development strategy will be required to impact directly on business performance. It would result in developing people with the skills and talent necessary to respond to the needs of the market place. John Horner, of Lombard Continental, put it simply:

The major challenge facing management development is to ensure that the organisation has the right people in the right place at the right time.

This view was strongly reinforced by Garrett Bouton of Scandinavian Bank:

Those concerned with human resource management have a responsibility, which goes beyond identifying and developing employee skills to the best advantage of the employee and the organisation at the present time. More importantly they have to ensure that people of the right quality and quantity will constantly be available to fulfil the requirements generated by the corporate plan of the organisation.

As well as meeting the requirements of the corporate plan, a number of organisations see specific, market-related, expectations. At the Nationwide Building Society, Jack Rutley sees a clear expectation that management development strategies will result in improved customer service skills:

The only thing that will differentiate retail financial services organisations will be its people – those in contact with the customer. There must be a customer focus. Effective customer service skills must be developed at all levels. We will know that we are achieving this if our customers initiate contact with the society, and have the view that our staff are professional and give better service than our competitors.

● *Management development strategy will result in adequate succession and continuity of management*

The need for resourcing to meet operational requirements leads to an expectation that the development strategy will incorporate effective manpower and succession planning procedures. The adequacy of succession plans, and availability of a pool of people to fill senior posts, is considered a good indicator as to whether or not the management development process has been successful.

The succession requirement goes beyond the static view of replacing existing jobholders with new ones in the same job. It is more concerned with having an adequate pool of skills and talent to provide the organisation with continuity in management able to respond to changing organisational and market needs. This pool should be able to both cover existing jobs, and contain the talent necessary to resource new, or expanded, business activity.

● *Management development strategy should increase the organisation's self-sufficiency in terms of human resources*

Closely linked to succession planning is an expectation that organisations will become increasingly self-sufficient in developing both specialist and managerial skills required to meet business needs.

This expectation is heightened by the increased competition for, and costs of, skilled people. In many organisations a major aim of management development strategy is seen as reducing the need to 'buy in' people at senior levels. This implies an expectation that the management development strategy will both reduce the loss of talented people as well as developing the skills required to meet current and future business needs.

● *Management development strategy will develop and reinforce corporate values*

Since the publication of *In Search of Excellence*, by Peters and Waterman, there has been a growing interest in corporate values and corporate culture. Steven Davis's book *Excellence in Banking* reinforces the significance of corporate values in the banking world. In many organisations in the financial sector, management development is seen as having to play a major role in disseminating and reinforcing corporate values. Donald Kirkham at the Woolwich expresses a typical view held by senior management in the sector:

At the Woolwich we clearly see being value driven as a distinctive feature of successful companies. We have a clear view of the values underpinning our business. It is essential that these values are effectively communicated and reinforced, and that their relevance is demonstrated through our development programmes.

Very closely associated with the communication of values is the expectation that effective management development, which is in itself value driven, will engender greater corporate loyalty. At a time of fierce competition for skilled people in the sector, the importance of developing increased corporate loyalty becomes increasingly significant.

● *Management development strategy will contribute to the effective management of change within the organisation*

One of the key issues facing businesses in the financial sector is the ever-increasing rate of change. To succeed in such an environment, organisations must become more flexible in terms of products, marketing strategies and the way in which they are structured and operate.

Underpinning the need for organisational flexibility is a need for organisational flexibility is a need for flexibility and responsiveness in management. There is a clear, and frequently explicit, expectation that management development programmes will be designed to ensure the provision of more flexible and responsive managers. Part of this process will entail helping managers to acquire the skills, and develop the broader business understanding, necessary to cope with greater devolution of responsibility and accountability.

All of this represents change. Change in the organisation, the manager's role, and the roles and methods of working with peers and subordinates. It is common that top management expect the management development strategy to result in improved management of change within the organisation.

One major change faced by most companies in the sector is that of expansion of product and service ranges. This gives rise to a need to effectively integrate new people, and/or new businesses into the organisation. This presents an expanded change management requirement which is probably at its most extreme in those organisations most directly affected by 'Big Bang'.

This challenge and expectation was clearly identified and expressed by Jeffrey Hernu of Barclays de Zoette Wedd:

Management development in Barclays de Zoette Wedd must make a major contribution to equipping our managers to manage change, and to affect a successful programme of integration, following the recent merger of disparate organisations and cultures.

The expectations summarised reflect top managements' concern with survival and growth in a competitive environment. Survival and growth is seen as requiring the development of managers who are resilient and responsive. There is a recognised need for people who are capable of rapid learning, who can cope with a diverse range of assignments and organisational structures, and who can work with a frequently changing group of colleagues.

This environment gives rise to an expectation that management development strategy will lead to the development of skilled managers able to operate in the new climate. It also leads to expectations of continued success in business operations, underpinned by ensuring that succession to key posts is effectively managed in a way which provides both continuity and quality in management.

CRITICAL SUCCESS FACTORS

Having obtained a clear and sharply focused picture of top management expectations of management development, the next stage is to identify the elements which are the key to fulfilling these expectations. The range of factors identified as being critical to the success of a management development strategy was diverse. However, a number of common factors, or themes, ran through this range. Those identified as core critical success factors are summarised below.

Identification of skills and talents

There are two distinct aspects to this factor. First, an effective strategy needs to identify the skills and talents needed to meet current and future business needs. This process must take account of changing requirements in terms of both new and obsolete skills. At the Midland this need is clearly recognised by Melvyn Howell:

It is vital that the skills required to compete effectively in a volatile market are clearly identified. It is equally important that redundant skills (resulting from change) are quickly recognised and acknowledged. In both cases the organisation's development programmes should be geared to reacting rapidly to the changing profiles. In today's environment, fast reaction to change is essential.

The second aspect of this factor is that an effective strategy must be built upon a good understanding of the skills and talents available within the organisation. This information and knowledge is, all too often, not readily available. The critical nature of this aspect was clearly identified by Jack Rutley of Nationwide:

The abilities of our staff are not really known. In the past this has not been important, as the business and structure of jobs have been relatively simple. Now, however, both the business and jobs are becoming increasingly complex. A better knowledge of the skills, talents, abilities and aspirations of our people is vital in order to achieve optimum performance.

There is overwhelming support for the view that an effective management development strategy must include clear profiles of the current and future skill requirements of the business. It must also include an inventory of available skills and talents and a mechanism for keeping both fully up to date.

Future looking

Implied in the above factor is the fact that development strategy is forward looking. Clear understanding of future skills is one key to success.

An effective management development strategy needs to be forward looking on a much broader front. It is essential that the strategy takes into account future business plans, product ranges, organisation structures, markets and resource requirements. This is a tall order in an environment where corporate planning is increasingly uncertain beyond a few years. The forward orientation is not judged by precision and accuracy of forecasts. Its importance, as a success factor, is more concerned with philosophy and adaptability. An effective management development strategy is one which recognises the uncertainty of the future, identifies core programmes and ensures that these can be readily modified to meet changing needs. Built around these core programmes are more flexible programmes designed to meet the differing and changing needs of the diverse range of business units in the organisation.

Business focused and responsive

It is essential that the management development strategy focuses on the real business needs of the overall organisation, and separate business units within it. This means that it may not be possible, or even desirable, to have a common programme applying to all parts of the organisation. It appears increasingly likely that success will result from having a number of strategies to meet the requirements of different units, or parts of the business, with an 'umbrella' strategy to meet the overall corporate needs.

It is essential that the strategy (or strategies) is kept under constant review to ensure that it is being adapted to meet changing business objectives and needs.

The management development programme must produce people with the skills and talents to grow and develop the business, rather than people equipped with a range of skills determined by a 'model' view of an effective manager. It is essential that the management development strategy produces resources to meet current and future operational requirements.

Involvement of line management

From the previous factor it becomes clear that it is essential that line management are actively involved in the formulation, and implementation, of management development strategy.

Indeed, given the general view on devolving accountability, it is likely that, increasingly, organisations will devolve accountability for management development to the heads of separate business units.

The Legal and General currently provide a good illustration of the move to making operational management responsible for management development focused on its own sphere of responsibility. Each subsidiary company is responsible for establishing and implementing its own operational management development strategy. Centrally the Group make available expertise, which may be drawn on as required. There is little intervention in the programmes operated in the subsidiaries, with group management assessing effectiveness in terms of succession continuity and performance. On top of individual subsidiary strategies, there is a group strategy. This is limited to ensuring that the needs of group management are effectively met, and is one area in which group requirements may take precedent over those of the subsidiary.

Many organisations see the involvement of line management as the most important of the critical success factors. Garrett Bouton of Scandinavian Bank sees this as critical, and also as a major change in the role of many line managers. In talking of the involvement of line management in the development process, he says:

This, during the next decade, will become one of the singularly most important factors in achieving excellence. For too long line managers have been judged against short term goals relating to productivity targets, problem solving or simply getting the job done.

Because of the rapidly changing environment it is going to be necessary for line managers to be actively involved in the people development process. They must be aware of the long term organisational goals and be made responsible for the development of their people. To achieve this it may be necessary to review the communication process within the organisations. It may also be necessary to review the appraisal process to ensure that managers, and their people, are targeted for longer-term development goals.

Effective communication

The effectiveness of management development is greatly enhanced if all involved are fully aware of the purposes, strategy and processes. The importance of communication in securing the involvement of line management was highlighted above. It is equally important that those who will be future managers have a clear understanding of the route to be followed, bases of decision-making, and importance of the process to the business overall.

As with any aspect of communication, it is important that it is two way and as open as possible. It is an important part of the design and implementation of development strategy that good communication is maintained with managers.

The detailed content of the strategy should be communicated as widely and openly as possible. Here there are clearly limitations. Few organisations disclose the detail of their top level succession plans. Within the sector, practice varies from merely disclosing that a plan exists to clearly communicating which people are in the 'succession pool'.

An important element in the communication process is ensuring a good flow of upward communication. This is particularly important in ensuring a clear view of individuals' aims and aspirations is developed. There is little point in having a person earmarked for a key post, or major developmental move, if they do not wish to move. Increasingly individual views on career development incorporate issues relating to quality of life.

Effective and open appraisal

The organisation's appraisal system plays an important part in obtaining information on individuals and in building, and maintaining, an inventory of skills, talents and aspirations. It also provides one important vehicle for ensuring effective communication of management development issues.

To contribute to the success of a management development strategy it is critical that the appraisal system is effective. The definition of what makes for an effective appraisal system is the subject for a book in its own right. Here the key elements may be summarised as:

- Clearly distinguishes between performance and potential. The record of performance in past jobs can be one of the most reliable indicators of skills and talents. This data should not be lost by merging it with what can often be a less reliable, and certainly more subjective, individual assessment of potential.
- Is based upon targets or objectives. This helps to ensure the validity of performance data and provides a mechanism for focused individual development.
- Is open and two way. It is important, as mentioned earlier, to ensure that the individuals' aspirations and interests are clearly established. In addition an open, two-way process helps to ensure that development issues are examined and discussed, and that plans are implemented.
- Is centrally monitored. There is a need to ensure that the data on individuals is 'captured' to enable the manpower inventory to be regularly updated and provide a valid basis for planning. It is

also useful to have a facility for reviewing consistency in standards and judgements, applied to both performance and potential.

Provides a pool of talent

Given the difficulty in arriving at a precise definition of the future nature and structure of jobs, it is seen as critical that the management development process provides a good 'pool' of talent. This pool may be drawn on to match the requirements of a job as it emerges. In this way the organisation is provided with a flexible resource bank. The flexibility is underpinned by the ability of the organisation to capitalise on the available talent by creating new jobs, structures, or even moving into new business areas to make full use of the skills and abilities presented.

This 'pool' approach enables the organisation to make the best use of its resources by effective person/job matching.

Provides an integrated strategy

The need for management development to be viewed in a far broader role than the 'traditional' training and education one was highlighted earlier in this chapter.

A critical success factor regularly identified is that management development strategy must cover many aspects of human resource management, and integrate action across a broad front. Increasingly issues such as reward policy, communication and performance evaluation are coming within the coverage of management development strategy.

SUMMARY

This chapter has examined the way in which views on the nature and scope of management development have changed in the light of the changes taking place in the financial sector. The major changes in views and perceptions may be summarised as:

● An increasing recognition of the importance of people in relation to the achievement of business goals.
● Management development has become a 'core' business issue and is no longer a peripheral activity.

- People can give a company a competitive edge.
- Escalating recruitment costs have highlighted the need for companies to develop their own skilled people.
- Squeezed margins highlight the need for productivity, and to treat investment in people with the same care as other investments.
- Management development strategy has to be an integral part of overall corporate planning.
- Management development is an issue of increasing concern at Chief Executive level.

These significant changes have given rise to a clear set of expectations in terms of what management development should deliver. These are:

- Assistance in improving business performance.
- Adequate succession and continuity of management.
- Increased self-sufficiency in terms of human resources.
- Development, dissemination and reinforcement of corporate values.
- Contribution to the effective management of change within the organisation.

To meet this set of expectations a range of critical success factors applying to the structuring and implementation of management development strategies has been identified. The 'core', or common, critical success factors were:

- Clear identification for skills and talents, both required and available.
- Strategy to be forward looking.
- Business focused and responsive to change.
- Involvement of line management.
- Effective communication.
- Effective and open appraisal.
- Provides a 'pool' of talent.
- Provides a strategy fully integrated with all human resource management policies.

The movement of management development from a 'nice to do' personnel function to a front line business issue has been argued as being a necessary one for a long time by personnel and management development specialists. Now that it is happening the pressure for real contributions to business performance will be high. The following chapters will examine how the desired results may be achieved, and identify the full range of thinking which will need to go into the formulation of future management development strategy.

4 The Way It Was

The preceding chapters have identified the nature and extent of the changes being faced by organisations in the financial sector. The changes in the nature of management jobs and skills required have been examined, together with the expectations that top management now have in relation to management development, and the factors considered to be critical to the success of a management development strategy.

In this chapter the traditional approaches to management development in the financial sector are examined. In looking at how development has commonly been approached, the relevance of these approaches to the current climate will be considered, together with the extent to which they have succeeded in meeting the needs of organisations in the past.

The approaches described tend to be those which have been dominant in the financial sector. Inevitably, in trying to present an overall picture, there is a danger of oversimplification through generalisation. There are companies in the sector who have already changed strategy and practice to meet the changing market needs. Many of these changes are described in later chapters. However, there are still a large number of companies operating very firmly within some of the traditional frameworks described. These companies will need to review and rethink their strategies if the management development processes to make a significant contribution to their overall business performance. For those already contemplating change, this chapter should provide some indicators of the direction in which any change should move.

PROMOTION AND CAREER DEVELOPMENT

Traditionally, within the financial sector, promotion has resulted from effective performance of a technical function. In some parts of the sector this practice is underpinned by a belief that the whole business is technically driven. For example, in some insurance organisations there is a view that a business does not need to invest energy or resources in management development. In these organisations there is often a generally based suspicion of any 'management techniques'.

However, in the sector overall, it has not purely been within these 'suspicious' companies that promotion practice has been driven by technical performance. In many companies where there has been investment in management training and education, the underlying promotion and career development practice has been technically driven.

Overall, investment in training and development has traditionally been strongly weighted in favour of technical training. The main aim of the development 'philosophy' has been to produce first class technicians and professionals.

David Woodward of Scandinavian Bank summarises the frequent outcome of this emphasis in development – and a common problem in the sector;

> Scandinavian Bank have been very good at developing bankers, but not so good at developing businessmen. In fact we have been so good at developing bankers that we often lose them to the competition.

Derek Day, of Alexander Howden, identifies another common problem with the technically-driven approach to career development:

> The succession process in insurance broking tends to result in organisations promoting people into management roles who do not appreciate the full responsibility of being a manager. The balance between being a competent broker and an effective manager is not naturally acquired.

This is by no means a phenomenon limited to insurance broking. In life assurance companies sales management has been beset with problems resulting from the promotion of successful salesmen to branch manager positions. This problem is now clearly recognised and the essentially different demands and skills of the two jobs are also recognised. Increasingly, companies are putting efforts into identifying and developing management skills, and modifying their approach to promotion and development, in the sales force. The realisation, initiated in the sales area, is now spilling over into other parts of these companies.

The example of problems resulting from technically-driven career development in the insurance industry is supported by direct parallels in both banking and building societies.

Promotion of excellent technicians to managerial positions is, in part, a direct result of unitary views on career and reward structures. Highly centralised organisations have tended to have a single path career structure. Managerial jobs have, generally, higher status and higher rewards. Thus the aspirations of staff are shaped towards upward progression. The reward for good performance has been regular promotion until the 'Peter' principle applies and performance plateaus or declines. This carries with it a further problem. People promoted to positions for which they are either unprepared or unsuited tend, due to the past 'paternalistic' culture in the sector, to stay put. This has resulted in career path blockages leading to either the loss, or gross under-utilisation, of skilled people at subordinate levels.

A shift away from technically-driven promotion cannot be effected successfully without making a fundamental change to the reward and career structures. There is a need to develop a structure which contains at least two promotion and reward routes. The technician, who either does not aspire to, or have the skills for, management, should be able to see a career path providing rewards, scope for fulfilment and standing in the organisation. Equally there is a need for a career path for those equipped to follow the managerial route. In practice, needs for other structures may also be evident.

Until this change in perception of promotion and career development occurs it is difficult to effectively plan a development strategy and determine the appropriate allocation of resources and priorities.

JOB-EXPERIENCE-BASED DEVELOPMENT

In many organisations, within the financial sector, there has been a recognition that *real* development is best achieved through job experience.

In the larger organisations in particular this view has resulted in policies of regularly moving those people perceived as having potential for further promotion and growth. The clearing banks in the UK have, in the past, provided a good example of this approach. It has not been uncommon for people to be moved every couple of years. These moves have often entailed major changes in the type of job being carried out, as well as changes in the branch, department or function.

Underlying this approach has been the view that the needs of the organisation are best met by developing breadth of experience, and producing good 'generalists' with a grasp of a wide range of the organisation's activities. As a result the organisation was frequently left with gaps in specialist functions, which inhibited the development of such functions, and has led to needs for external recruitment. When external recruitment has taken place, the organisation has not had the depth of cover. A further problem related to this approach is that it can lead to a lack of longer-term continuity in functional and operational management, particularly at junior and middle management levels.

The relatively short periods worked in jobs has tended to militate against delegation of real accountability and responsibility, thus reinforcing the strong centralisation of decision-making.

The insurance industry has also had a tendency to look at job experience as a major strand in development strategies. However, movement around departments or functions has been more limited to the early stages of careers. Specialisation has tended to occur at a relatively early point. This has resulted in problems in developing sufficiently broad managers to fill senior vacancies, and created a number of succession problems.

Building societies also place a premium on job-based development. In these organisations the branch network is the main focus of development strategy. Development programmes are primarily aimed at developing branch managers. It is the pool of branch management which is generally looked to to provide resources to fill head office management functions. While the business remained relatively simple this has produced a reasonably satisfactory arrangement. However, the growth in the complexity of the business is giving rise to an increasing need for head office specialists, and an increasing level of demands on head office management. The need for more managerial input in head office cannot continue to be met by depleting branch resources. There is a recognition that strategies will have to be evolved to provide for better development within head office departments and functions.

The UK clearing banks have had a strong, centrally-managed, policy on job experience and movement as part of the development process. Due to the strong central policy, job movement has occurred and been an accepted (if not appreciated) practice by management.

In the insurance industry the aim of developing managers through varied job experience has often been difficult to achieve in practice. David Salmon of the Chartered Insurance Institute clearly identified the problem in the industry:

> Many of the *real* development possibilities, in terms of building experience through a range of jobs, have been hampered by line managers' ability to 'hold on' to good people to meet short term, parochial needs.

A general problem with the job-experience-based approach to management development is that the actual experience gained, and pattern of job moves, is unplanned and distorted by operational needs, or availability of openings. Where this approach is underpinned by planned 'models' of career paths it can be effective. In such cases, however, the planning is often based upon historical perspectives of the experience required to equip a person for senior managerial positions. This planning framework is unlikely to be effective in today's volatile environment.

GENERIC SKILLS DEVELOPMENT

The financial sector has seen a considerable expansion of management training and education over the last 20 years. Indeed, in many organisations in the sector, the approach to management development has been almost exclusively based upon management training and education. The strategy upon which training and education has been based may best be described as one geared to developing generic management skills which, having been mastered, equip a manager to operate effectively in any situation. Whilst this may be oversimplifying the strategies employed, it is clear that major investment of resources, time and energy has been invested in generic training and education programmes.

This core skills approach tends to apply to most levels of management. At the middle to senior level of management, extensive use tends to be made of business schools with programmes designed to impart general management skills. At lower levels, programmes ranging from supervisory skills through to specific 'techniques' (for example, time management, appraisal interviewing) proliferate. Extensive use of 'public' programmes, open to participants from a diverse range of companies and sectors, has generally been found to have little impact on meeting the real needs of organisations in the sector for developing managerial talent. To overcome the lack of results, there has been a growing tendency to bring the training and education in-house, either by recruiting specialist trainers or by using external specialists. In the opinion of many, whilst this change brings some improvements in short-term results, it still fails to address the real management development issues and needs.

John Skae, of Legal and General, clearly identified a problem with the generic approach:

> At the Legal and General we have found that the generic-skills-based and 'macro' management development programmes cannot cope in times of rapid change and uncertainty.
>
> A major problem arises when you cannot clearly see what is going to happen in the future. In such a case there is no point in trying to impose a 'macro' development or hypothesis.

At the Midland Bank, Melvyn Howell sees the change in operating environment as invalidating the traditional, generic-skills-based, approach:

> The sharpening of decision-making processes and structures represents a major cultural change in the UK clearing banks. Traditionally the banks' approach to developing managers has been on a highest common factor basis, linked with a philosophy of developing generalists. This approach has to change to support the sharper decision-making structure, and ensure that talent and potential is fully utilised and focused on achieving business objectives.

Brian Chandler, Director of Training at the accounting firm Arthur Young, feels strongly that the generic skills approach is irrelevant. He bases his views on both what he observes in the accountancy profession, and his direct experience of 'being developed' within such a framework:

> The idea of a common body of management skills is a myth. In

my experience of programmes built on this idea, knowledge is acquired within a framework which suggests an 'ideal' end result. In reality people need to be taught how to learn and how to adapt the changing environments. The concept of a common body of knowledge is merely an academic, and convenient, framework for packaging and delivering training.

The 'generic skills' approach to management development has been expensive, and seen as failing to produce managers with the skills needed in the sector in sufficient volumes. The limitations of this approach are by no means confined to the financial sector. J. M. Harries, writing in *Training and Development* ('Should Management Development be a Three Way Contract?' – July 1986) provides a good summary of the problems and limitations:

> It is our assertion that we need to take a holistic view of the contribution which training and development can make to British management practice. Until now we have, very largely, taken the opposite stance: one of throwing a mass of approaches, theories and techniques at managers in the hope that enough of them will stick. Thus we have a plethora of organisations in the business of management development.

He then goes on to consider the results of the investment in this approach:

> But, here again, one must pose the seminal question: where is the objective evidence that all this provision, much of it highly expensive, is making a measurable contribution to improved managerial effectiveness?

It is this question which is increasingly being asked in the financial sector. The common skills approach suffers from one major deficiency. The provision of training based upon the generic assumptions tends to be largely theory driven. The 'models' provide a tidy view of management which does not match with reality. The theoretical model portrays managers as operating, using skills of planning, directing and co-ordinating. In reality, managers work in a fragmented and untidy way. The observation of the way in which managers operate was well described by Bill Braddick of Ashridge, writing in the *Journal of European Industrial Training* (July 1984):

Those who work with managers know that they enjoy working under pressure. They like deadlines and set them for themselves if none exist. They are impatient with abstractions. They like to solve real problems; they want something they can get their teeth into.

He goes on to highlight the problems with the training which is provided for current and potential managers:

Yet the design of the traditional executive development programme, with its plethora of cases, reliance on the written word, its leisurely abstraction, its concern for conceptualisation and generalisation reflects the learning needs of the academic teacher far more than those of the typical manager with his concerns for the real and the immediate.

Overall, within the financial sector, the generic-skills-based approach to development, with its emphasis on training and development, has been the predominant one. In many cases the only development activity has been the provision of training and education. There is now a realisation that this approach is not producing the skills required. More is needed. Where training and education is to play a role it must move from being based upon academic models of how a manager works, to being based upon reality. Training and education must be geared to providing managers with the skills and understanding necessary to them to cope with a changing and uncertain environment.

CREATING OPPORTUNITIES

A number of the 'younger', and fast growth, organisations in the financial sector have, in the past, had a philosophy of 'self-selection' development. In some cases these may be seen as a 'jungle'-based approach to development, in which the fittest survive and rise to senior posts in the organisation. The 'jungle' approach is, in essence, *laissez faire*. It may be seen as ignoring the need to take positive action to develop managerial skills and talents. In some companies in the sector there is little doubt that this is the case.

However, some organisations have had a 'self-selection' approach as a planned policy. Allied Dunbar (formerly Hambro Life) have traditionally operated a development policy based upon the creation of opportunities for people to grow. The emphasis has been on creating an environment in which people are encouraged to develop themselves. This has entailed developing job structure with real accountability and delegation of authority. Success is usually well rewarded and training support often demand based.

This policy has been largely successful to date. The stage reached in the organisation's growth, and changes in the market, now lead Allied Dunbar to recognise the need to formalise this development process. The challenge, in the view of Peter Russell of Allied Dunbar, is:

> To formalise the approach to management development without losing the flexibility we currently enjoy and without losing the entrepreneurial spirit and skills currently developed in our successful managers.
>
> A major problem encountered in the past has been the inability to produce good branch managers in the quantity needed. The good salesmen do not always select to go into management. Those that do, do not always make good managers. This is where the need for a greater degree of formalisation of an intervention in the development process is becoming increasingly important.

Citicorp provides another good example of the 'self-selection' approach to development. Malcolm Parker, of Citicorp, describes their view of development in terms of creating opportunities and a personal growth environment:

> Due to its size and geographic spread, what Citicorp can offer is a good internal labour market. The environment is strong in terms of providing opportunity and challenge. This means that people can effectively change jobs without impacting on pension rights and without changing employers.
>
> Currently the identification of potential is largely informal. In Citicorp, potential often emerges as a result of 'delivery and push'. Individuals position themselves to take advantage of opportunities. Those who consistently 'deliver and push' get on.

Like Peter Russell at Allied Dunbar, Malcolm Parker sees a need to introduce a greater degree of structure and formalisation into the management development process. He sees a need for a better system of information and greater degree of intervention in order to meet the demand for future managerial skills and talents.

'HOME-GROWN'-APPROACH

Approaches to management development in the financial sector have traditionally been strongly underpinned by a philosophy of 'growing our own skills and talents'. The increasing need for external recruitment indicates that the aims of this philosophy are no longer being fully realised. Approaches to development have not succeeded in responding quickly enough to embryonic changes in needs, resulting from changes in market conditions.

The 'grow our own' philosophy has led to a long-term view on development. The pool from which future talent will emerge has been replenished each year by school- or university-leaver recruitment. In many organisations this recruitment has been indiscriminate. It has merely been based on recruiting a volume of people, with a defined level of qualifications, to feed into the organisation. In practice, recruitment has taken place at a mixture of entry points (that is, 16-plus, GCE 'A' level leavers and graduates). All have been seen as being potentially capable of eventually moving into management. The 'general's baton' philosophy has impacted on development strategy. Every entrant is a potential chief executive!

This philosophy has resulted in a 'leisurely' approach to development, with little focus in terms of the organisation's needs. Melvyn Howell of the Midland sees the need to sharpen the development process, resulting in a need to start with recruitment:

> The traditional undiscriminated approach to recruitment has to be replaced by one much more objectively based, and strategically targeted.

The 'grow our own' philosophy, particularly in the larger organisations, has tended to lead to a development process which is unfocused and unrelated to business needs; or related to an historic picture of the nature and demands of management jobs.

Harry Broomhead (Group Personnel Manager of the Royal Insurance Group) summarised the past approach both in the Royal and the insurance sector as a whole:

The Royal has always been regarded as being pretty good at all forms of training. However, in retrospect, it has to be acknowledged that the development effort has lacked really critical direction. Whilst it has been excellent in bringing on a very small number of career staff who are now senior managers, it has otherwise tended to be a policy of development per se, rather than development for a clear purpose. I think it has really lacked a clear perspective about demand and supply. As a result we have not produced all the skills and talents required to meet the needs of a changing environment.

There is now a recognition that the 'grow our own' philosophy is important. The need to develop skills and avoid the disruptive, and expensive, process of large-scale external recruitment is felt to be critical in the future. However, in the past, 'growing our own' has led to an inbred organisation, slow to respond to change. In the future the philosophy will have to be supported by a greater sensitivity to the external environment, and a recognition of the need to bring in 'new blood' from time to time. The philosophy will have to be backed by a more sharply focused approach to recruitment and development. Volatile and competitive financial markets will result in the destruction of the comfortable business environment which has supported the past approaches.

MECHANISTIC SUCCESSION PLANNING

Much of the development activity in the sector has been based upon a view of the nature and structure of management jobs, and the organisation, which is derived from the jobs as currently or historically defined.

It is this view of jobs which has underpinned views on the skills, talents and experience which need to be developed to provide for succession.

Where succession planning has been actively employed as a part of the development strategy, it has tended to be built on a 'steady state' view of the organisation. Succession plans have largely focused on providing replacements for current jobs. It has been a fairly mechanistic process. The starting point has been internally focused with an objective of filling jobs: a process of 'putting names to boxes'. The 'static' model upon which plans have been based has failed to take account of the way in which the organisation, the structure of jobs and the skills required have needed to change to respond to market conditions. As a result, the development process has frequently failed to produce people capable of dealing with the challenges facing the business. In the earlier, comfortable, and relatively stable business environment, the steady state and mechanistic approach to succession planning contributed to the continuation of the organisational style and structure. It provided a degree of stability and continuity. However, even in relatively slowly changing conditions, this mechanistic succession planning led to failures in developing the skills required in senior positions.

In the current climate, failure to meet succession and continuity needs can lead to significant, and far-reaching, problems for an organisation.

The changing environment requires a move away from mechanistic succession planning. This mechanistic approach has been described in terms of having 'boxes looking for names to fill them'. In the view of Melvyn Howell of the Midland, failure to change this will have serious consequences, beyond those of succession itself:

> Simplistic succession planning is structure driven. If implemented it would tend to build rigidity into the organisation, but in reality it is likely to be over-ridden by 'ad-hoc' selection decisions. To be effective in the current, rapidly changing climate, succession planning needs to be flexible, robust and closely linked to organisation development.

In organisations where there has been no real formalised succession planning, the approaches to management development have been driven by assumptions about the nature of jobs, and experience routes, necessary to provide for succession.

For example, in many of the larger building societies traditional career development has tended to be from branch management into head office management, and from there into senior management. The nature and shape of the overall structure of the organisation and the senior management jobs has been considered as being relatively stable. In a situation where the societies' business remained relatively simple, and protected, the basic assumptions on which development was built were valid. Succession, by and large, was not an issue. However, their environment is changing as rapidly as that for others in the sector. The 'traditional' assumptions will no longer hold, significant changes in development strategy will be necessary.

IDENTIFICATION OF POTENTIAL

'Traditional' indiscriminate approaches to recruitment have frequently been accompanied by a relatively unstructured approach to the identification of those with potential for development and promotion. Where there is a systematic attempt at the identification of potential, it has tended to be focused on the organisation's appraisal system. In many cases the distinction between assessment of performance and potential has been somewhat blurred.

Many appraisal systems, in use in the financial sector, have tended to be very trait orientated. Managers have been asked to make judgements on personality traits such as perseverence, enthusiasm and initiative of their subordinates. The value of such approaches has become increasingly questionable. Problems identified have related to both the ambiguity of the terminology and the subjectivity of the judgement. There has, for some time now, been a move to separation of the assessment of performance from that of potential.

In terms of performance appraisal, there is a continuing increase in the use of objectively-based systems relating to target achievement and fulfilment of job accountabilities. This is improving the quality of information of people's past performance. However, assessment of potential, in many cases, remains subjective and unfocused.

In spite of moving towards more objectively-based appraisal, the links between the appraisal systems and management development strategies are often weak. The most common use of appraisal remains that associated with reward. All too frequently managers' perceptions of the appraisal process are related to its use as a vehicle for determining salary increases, and movement through salary scales.

Links with the management development process tends to focus on two areas, viz.:

● Identification of training needs
● Suitability for promotion

Identification of training needs is frequently a 'menu' approach. A list of available courses is provided and appraisers tick those perceived as relevant to the person being appraised. The problem presented by this approach is two-fold. First, there is a tendency to 'tick a course' purely because it is felt to be a 'good idea', or because it is 'about time for some training'. In other words it often results in training for its own sake rather than training to meet specific need or objective. Secondly, the range of courses offered tends to reflect a generic view of development needs. In fact this approach is very common in organisations with a 'generic skills' view of management development.

The perceived advantage of the 'box ticking' identification of training needs is that it makes the co-ordination of information easier to handle. It is an approach which eases the planning of training activities. However, its contribution to providing development suited to the current and future needs of the business is often perceived as being minimal.

A common alternative to the 'menu' approach to training needs identification is the open question, inviting the appraiser's assessment of training required. This presents problems in handling the responses and ensuring that the training, identified as being necessary, is provided.

The manager making an appraisal is often asked to make a judgement on the individual's suitability for further promotion. This is frequently related to a potential assessment. The main problems, with this aspect of the appraisal, arise due to the manager's lack of knowledge of the demands and needs of the business in terms of jobs available. Judgements tend to be based upon a limited perception of career paths, and an historic picture of job structures and demands.

Overall, in relation to management development, appraisal systems have not been effectively used. However, they can potentially play an important role in a management development strategy. To do so it is necessary to use them as a source of past performance data, and to ensure that appraisers are provided with a clear understanding of the skills and talents which are going to be needed in the organisation. In this way a movement towards obtaining improved information on potential within the organisation may be made.

Although a lot of organisations in the financial sector have made use of appraisal systems as part of their overall approach to management development, many have recognised their shortcomings. A significant number use appraisal data as only one of a range of inputs into the identification of potential. In other organisations either no formal appraisal system exists, or the system has become little more than a mechanical exercise which is ignored, or seen as having no relevance to the business and its development needs. However, most organisations who have recognised the critical future role of management development, also recognise the need for good information on performance and potential to underpin development strategies.

Jack Rutley, of the Nationwide Building Society, sees knowledge of people as a key ingredient in management development:

> There is a real need to know more about our staff. Currently insufficient is known and the optimum job matches are not realised. Potential is not always identified and there is a feeling that staff could be better employed.

Nationwide's current approach to identification of potential is similar to that used by many organisations in the financial sector. It is a combination of obtaining information from appraisal forms, together with reports and comments from managers. Generally the focus of managers' reports tends to be on past performance. This is widely seen as being a reliable indicator of potential.

An organisation's overall development philosophy influences its approach to the identification of potential. The generic skills approach tends to be associated with appraisal systems and/or managerial reports on past performance, leading to trait-based potential assessment. On the other hand, organisations such as Allied Dunbar and Citicorp rely on individuals taking the initiative in putting themselves in a position to be seen as having development potential. In organisations such as these there is an increasing recognition of the need to introduce a degree of structure into the identification of potential. The need for information on people is seen as important in improving the process of development, and ensuring that future needs are effectively met.

Accurate identification of potential will become increasingly important in the management development process. This will give rise to a need, in many organisations, to change their approach. The change will need to be towards a more focused process. Identification of potential will need to be related to a clear understanding of the future skills and talents required in different jobs throughout the organisation. Once the question 'potential for what?' has been answered, the means of identification of potential may be addressed.

An increasing number of organisations are addressing the means and moving to the use of techniques such as testing and assessment centres. However, few companies have formalised the process of building job and skill profiles of future management jobs. It is only by developing a clear future skills profile that a development strategy, which will make a real contribution to the business, may be established.

PROBLEMS WITH 'TRADITIONAL' APPROACHES

A number of problems associated with the traditional approaches to management development have been identified as each approach has been examined. In addition to those problems, already identified, there are a number of further common problems. Before reviewing these individually, it is worth restating that the most important overall problem is that, by and large, these approaches have failed to produce managers with the skills required in sufficient volumes. This has resulted in difficulties with succession and continuity, and a need to engage in expensive external recruitment.

Underpinning this overall problem are the following specific problems:

● *Lack of integration with business needs and plans*

In many instances management development has lacked a clear focus. The strategy has not been clearly related to the needs of the business and the changing demands resulting from changes in the external environment. There has been a tendency for development to be undertaken for its own sake, or because it is perceived to 'be a good thing', rather than to meet clearly-identified current and future business needs.

As a result of this lack of focus, management development has not been perceived as a significant activity by line managers. The consequent lack of commitment has further aggravated the lack of effectiveness of traditional approaches.

● *Raised expectations*

Credibility of, and commitment to, management development programmes has been damaged as a result of artificially raised expectations. On the one side, the investment of resources has often taken place in the hope that management development would contribute to the resolution of business problems. The anticipated results have not materialised, often due to lack of strategic direction of the process, and thus damaged credibility with senior management.

In the previous, comfortable, environment people became used to regular promotion. This upward mobility has tended to be linked with attending training programmes, and assessment of potential. Changes in the financial markets, and the introduction of technology, have removed many promotion opportunities. As a result the traditional correlation of training and potential assessment has disappeared. This has led to frustration and cynicism as the raised expectations, engendered by previous practice, have not been met.

Overall then there is often a perception that management development is a wasteful, or irrelevant, activity contributing neither to business nor individual needs.

● *Inhibiting change*

The fact that many management development programmes are built on a historic perception of jobs and organisation structure, and designed to promote associated skills, can establish a barrier to change in the group having been through the programme.

The dangers of developing people into a set mould are prevalent with the generic skills approach.

Jack Rutley has identified this problem at Nationwide and is sure that it is a common one:

A problem faced in developing people in Nationwide, and surely throughout the sector, is that managers in their thirties are often reluctant to accept change. We have fallen into the trap of moulding managers into a set pattern. Once established it is difficult to break the mould. Problems are increasingly arising when external forces demand a change.

In most organisations in the sector, problems of introducing and managing the change necessary to respond to fundamental market changes abound. It is clear that, in many of these organisations, the past approach to management development has built barriers to change rather than stimulate flexibility and adaptability. The problem cannot be laid entirely at the feet of management development. The culture of these organisations has imported the values of stability, predictability and observation of precedent, which have been reinforced by the development strategy.

SUMMARY

Although practice in relation to management development varies widely in the financial sector, it is possible to identify a range of core elements common in what may be termed 'the traditional approach'. These elements do not exist in isolation. In many organisations a number of them are combined in the overall strategy. The common elements identified were:

● Promotion based upon technical performance.
● Job experience as a significant part of development.
● Development based upon core skill, or generic, models of management.
● Development based upon the creation of opportunities, with onus on the individual to seize such opportunities as becoming available.
● An overall 'grow our own' philosophy underpinning management development strategy.
● Mechanistic succession planning, based on a historic view of job structures, demands and career paths.
● Identification of potential, based upon appraisal systems and managerial judgement, which is subjective and lacks focus in terms of the needs of the organisation.

The overall problem associated with the traditional approaches to management development is that they have failed to produce managers with the skills required to succeed in a volatile and competitive environment in sufficient numbers. This has resulted from a range of specific problems, including:

– Lack of integration of management development with the business strategy.
– Raised expectations of senior management and staff which have not been fulfilled.
– Inhibiting change by purveying values associated with a stable and predictable environment.

The challenges of the current environment clearly call for a change from the traditional approaches. The need for a shift from traditional processes is not confined to the financial sector. The need, and the problems to be overcome, have been clearly identified and summarised by John Davies and Yvonne Deigham ('The Managerial Menopause', *Personnel Management*, March 1986):

> To achieve the shift from the traditional decision process to the new one requires considerable effort. There is a growing awareness of some of the tasks that have to be done. One senior executive was adamant:
>
> > We need to have clearer and more precise assessments of the potential of managers. If people have a clearer idea of what they can do, of what is involved in the jobs above them and of what they could get out of their present jobs, then they can tailor their ambitions and potential to what is available. This may help with frustrations based on unrealistic expectations.

To meet this requirement means solving some long-standing and difficult problems of management development:

● Finding reliable and accurate predictive assessment techniques.
● Making appraisal work and linking it with self-development.
● Designing remuneration systems which reward people for what they do, rather than for where they are in the system.
● Producing training which helps managers do their jobs, rather than presenting them with ideals and models of managing (which can have the effect of reinforcing a sense of failure).
● Creating management systems which are not only committed to achieving business objectives, but which also aim to reflect the values of the people who work within them.

The list of problems, identified in this chapter, provides a framework for action and change.

Traditionally, financial sector organisations have tended to assimilate external change by means of incremental change in their own organisation and behaviour. The nature and extent of change in the current environment must call into question the continuation of an incremental change system. The need is for radical change. Increasingly organisations need to be able to respond rapidly to significant shifts in the external environment. This need implies a major shift in the approach to formulating and implementing management development strategy.

5 The Importance of Culture

In the previous chapter traditional approaches to management development were examined, and the problems and limitations associated with them identified. What is clear is that an organisation's approach to management development is significantly affected by its culture and value systems.

This chapter reviews the cultures commonly encountered in the financial sector and examines the ways in which these impact on management development strategy. The need for changes in cultures and value systems, in order to cope with the changing environment, is also examined. Some thoughts on how changes in culture may be effected are presented towards the end of the chapter.

COMMON CULTURES

It is virtually impossible to generalise about cultures in a sector which encompasses such a diverse range of organisations. However, accepting that some organisations differ significantly, it is possible to identify some 'models' which apply, to a large extent, in many of the organisations.

David Salmon of the Chartered Insurance Institute provided a clear picture of the 'traditional' insurance organisation culture:

> The 'traditional' approach to the insurance business has tended to result in organisation structures and cultures which under-utilise the potential and talents of their people. The levels of profits have led to total remuneration packages which are attractive. This, combined with a 'job for life' philosophy, has enabled over recruitment (in terms of qualification) to take place.

Within what David Salmon is saying, and observation of many insurance organisations, the key elements in their overall culture have tended to be:

● A 'job for life' philosophy. People join the organisation on leaving school, or college, and leave on retirement, having progressed through the organisation in a career path best suited to their talents.

● Generous remuneration policy geared to providing progressive salary and benefits over a long career cycle.

● Lack of real delegation of authority. Strongly centralised decision-making processes with delegation taking place within relatively tight guidelines, procedures and checks and balances.

● A 'grow our own talent' philosophy. Recruitment normally takes place at the school/college leaver level. Senior technical and managerial posts are filled from within the organisation.

● 'We look after our people'. The culture of insurers has often been described as being paternalistic. There has, in the past, been a clear value system based upon an implied exchange of commitments. In return for the joiners' loyalty and commitment to the organisation, the organisation is committed to looking after the joiner in terms of providing training, career opportunities, reward and benefits. The paternalistic approach has implied a reluctance to fire those who do not perform. To protect against non-performance, checks and balances are applied to operational decision-making.

Against this background it is not surprising to find approaches to management development which include regular job changes, 'steady state' perception of job requirements, and a large input of generic-skills-based management training.

In many cases the 'job for life' philosophy also carried with it a 'general's baton' view on career development. That is to say, every joiner is a potential Chief Executive. I can certainly recall working with one company in which the Chief Executive has worked his way up from the post room. In his opinion he has learned a lot from this process and viewed it as a 'norm', in terms of (at least) the starting point for any new entrant, however well qualified.

In practice the preceding summary presents a largely historical profile of cultures within the insurance business. Changes in the operating environment have driven changes in the culture. However, these cultures did exist for a long time (and still do on some companies) and although they may have changed, the approaches to management development are still affected by their residual influence.

Cultures in insurance broking have tended to be predominantly paternalistic and autocratic. This is a result of the fact that many brokers grew from relatively small family firms. Although they have grown significantly in size, the initial cultures have frequently survived to some degree.

The components of culture found in large insurance companies are also found when looking at the large UK clearing banks. Due to their size, and influence on the market, many of the smaller banks have tended to import elements of their culture. The main influence on the clearers' cultures has been that of the retail part, or division, of the bank. As with the historic profile of an insurance company, the typical bank culture has been dominated by over-recruiting, a 'job for life' philosophy, bureaucratic centralised controls and procedures to protect against error, with resulting failure to delegate real accountability and authority.

Once again, as with insurers, the cultures in banks are beginning to change. However, due to the size (particularly of the clearers), the pace of change is somewhat slower. Certainly the dismantling and refocusing of management development policies and structures will present a real challenge if a rapid change is required.

The traditional internal culture described for banks and insurers may be seen as being focused on processes and not results. It was the process of decision-making that typically warranted attention. Equally it was the process of management development which warranted attention. Increasingly, in the sector, there has been an emergence of organisations where the focus is reversed. It is results and not processes that are important. Organisations in which this cultural norm dominates have, in many instances, been outstanding in terms of their growth and performance

In these organisations the culture tends to be clearly articulated and widely understood. Peter Russell describes the situation in Allied Dunbar:

In Allied Dunbar the core culture is sales and service driven. The message to all is clear: 'Do it right. Do it now.'

The organisation is a sales one. The ability to deliver an efficient and effective service is the key to success. We could very effectively be selling any product. Given this focus, the organisation perceives both its salesforce and its policyholders as its customers.

In practice Allied Dunbar's values are expressed in a published policy statement, expressing the organisation's commitment to service and to its people. Peter Russell sees the strong culture being reinforced by the company's success and its growth record. He also recognises that the culture plays a major role in shaping the company's approach to management development.

Citicorp have a record of success and innovation. Malcolm Parker, of Citicorp Investment Bank, puts this down to their corporate culture:

> We have a track record of innovation, and actively foster a climate in which people are encouraged to try new things. The organisation is not afraid of mistakes and has the capital base to back 'trying things out'.
>
> The culture is meritocratic. It attracts and holds people who are interested in that style.

Again at Citicorp the culture impacts on the approach to management development. The underlying philosophy is:

> We will provide the opportunity which will help you to develop. But, it is up to you to take it and make something of it.

Malcolm Parker sees Citicorp's culture as action based, encouraging decision-making rather than consensus seeking. This is a typical emphasis in organisations concerned with results rather than processes. In contrast to the traditional cultures, outlined earlier, the culture in these organisations is characterised by extensive delegation of real accountability and authority and maximum exploitation of the available skills and talents of their people.

In such organisations the attitude towards devolution of authority, and encouraging autonomy, was summarised in a comment by David Woodward of Scandinavian Bank:

> In recent strategic planning meetings, the managing director has, in essence, said to the heads of business units: 'It is your business; go ahead and run it'.
>
> This philosophy is being supported by a reward structure highly geared towards the achievement of results.

Traditional insurance and banking cultures, and the results focused cultures, represent the extremes of a spectrum found in this part of the sector. Many organisations are in the process of moving along the spectrum. The results focused culture is associated with successful performance. However, its wholesale and unadapted importation into organisations, with an historically different culture, may well give rise to more problems than could potentially be solved.

In reviewing existing cultures, no mention has yet been made of building societies. Due to their somewhat 'special' historical origins they are considered separately.

CULTURE IN BUILDING SOCIETIES

Building societies originated as mutual organisations, developed to aid their members move into home ownership. This origin has had a major impact on culture and value systems in these organisations. To an extent the values of thrift and home ownership, on which societies were built, became formally encapsulated in the protective legislation governing their operation.

The Building Societies Act, which came into force on 1 January 1987, has significantly changed the status of societies by deregulating many of their activities. This change, which is ultimately reflecting market changes and competitive growth in the financial sector, looks as if it may present some in this market with something of an 'identity crisis'.

Societies look as if they will split into two (probably unequal) groupings. One group look likely to adhere to the traditional culture and value systems, whilst the other are looking to (and in some cases beginning to) develop a more commercially-driven culture and value system. To be completely accurate a third group should be highlighted. This group will comprise those societies which have just not considered the impact of the changes in markets and legislation on their culture.

Where culture has been recognised as being an issue, there is generally agreement that it is inexorably linked with the public image of the organisation.

Dennis Brockwell, of the Nationwide Building Society, identifies the key elements in their culture and value systems, as being:

● Doing their best for developing housing in the UK
● Social conscience
● Efficiency

● Providing the best service for their customers
● Providing a 'good deal' for staff

To an extent he feels that, in reviewing their strategy to deal with a changing market, Nationwide had 'rediscovered its roots'. This rediscovery has commercial implications. The recent advertising slogan using the expression 'put the building back into society' shows how Nationwide are promoting one of their traditional values as a competitive selling point.

The importance of traditional values is strongly supported by Donald Kirkham of the Woolwich Equitable Building Society:

> Here we are convinced that the values underpinning building societies have contributed strongly to their growth and development. I am convinced that adherence to these values will continue to provide us with a basis for further growth.

Like Dennis Brockwell of Nationwide, Donald Kirkham sees social responsibility as dominant in the Woolwich value systems:

> Our staff see themselves as being in a 'social services' business. This underpins our external image of being 'fair, friendly and approachable'. This is a competitive advantage that we would not wish to lose.

To Donald Kirkham, one of the critical aspects of the legislative changes is the facility to convert from mutual to public limited company status. He sees mutual status as significant. Any change would, inevitably, in his view, move the culture from being value driven to being profit driven.

Peter Birch of the Abbey National does not see this conflict. He is an advocate of moving societies to public limited company status. He sees such a move as essential, if societies are to be able to compete effectively with the other financial sector organisations. However, Peter Birch's view of the internal culture of the Abbey National encompasses many traditional elements. In particular, he sees it as a caring climate. It is seen as such by staff in practice. He summarises the other elements in the Abbey's culture, as follows:

> It is a progressive organisation which looks after its people well. Commitment and involvement is needed and actively sought at all levels. Customer service is a key value driving our organisation.

Crawford Laughlan, of the Halifax, sees culture and values as important in terms of the way in which staff maintain a society's public image:

> Building societies are heavily reliant on the quality of its people in the field. It is these people that the customers see, and through these people that the society's public image is developed and maintained.

He sees the biggest cultural change, being faced by building societies, as the change to a sales orientation.

The culture at the Nationwide, as described by Jack Rutley, has elements common in many traditional banking and insurance organisations:

> The current culture is one of 'cradle to grave' employment. Little external recruitment takes place at senior levels and our management development is underpinned by a 'grow our own' philosophy.

The need to bring in outside specialists to deal with new services is, in many societies, not significantly changing the 'grow our own culture'. It is common practice for societies to recruit externally the specialist to head up a new function and to have existing staff retrained to fill supporting roles.

In spite of adherence to traditional values, the Woolwich has developed an element of culture which earlier in this chapter was identified as characteristic of dynamic and successful banks and insurers. Donald Kirkham describes this aspect of the Woolwich Culture as follows:

> We have developed, and communicated, a strong value to the effect that learning through mistakes is the driving force which keeps an organisation responsive and adaptive.

In the current market, there is general agreement that the past conservatism of building societies has been a strength. This needs to be adapted in a way which retains the image of prudence and security without it becoming a major weakness. Innovation must be encouraged whilst retaining public confidence and trust.

ORGANISATION AND STRUCTURE

To a large extent the culture and values of organisation in the financial sector are reflected in their approach to organisation and structure.

Those organisations which have a traditional culture tend to be highly centralised. Policies, procedures and checks and balances are developed and controlled within the centre of the organisation. This is where the power lies and is the focal point of development strategies. Moving out and down from the centre, there is increasingly limited delegation of real decision-making power and authority.

With this centralised structure there is a strong reinforcement of a culture which is intended to apply throughout the organisation.

Organisations with a culture promoting active decision-making and delegation of real autonomy and accountability are increasingly moving towards a separate business unit organisation strategy. Each unit is relatively autonomous, within overall corporate performance targets and requirements. With this autonomy goes an acceptance that different units, dealing with different products, and operating in different segments of the market, will develop cultures and values appropriate to their sphere of operation.

To prevent complete 'cultural anarchy', these organisations tend to work actively to promote overall corporate culture and values which may be integrated with those predominant in the business units.

The legal structure (that is, holding company and subsidiaries or divisions within a company) is not as important as the organisational philosophy. What is important is that companies should recognise that their organisational structure and dominant culture and values are entwined. For example, a highly-centralised company, with decision-making and power focused in the centre, would find it difficult to promote a culture implying full exploitation and development of all individuals' skills and talents.

To effect major shifts in culture often requires the organisation to develop a structure which supports the new culture. The Legal and General provides a good example of the vital links between culture and structure. Legal and General moved from a fairly centralised structure, through a process of decentralisation and divisionalisation, to their current holding company and subsidiary structure. Accompanying this organisational change has been a change in culture from a traditional, limited delegation and limited risk one, to a high delegation one, with focus on results and not processes.

This example should be considered in the light of the motivation for change. Change was business driven. There was a recognition that the different parts of the business were operating in different markets and, to be successful, needed to be able to respond differently to meet the needs of, and complete effectively in, those markets. What the example does illustrate is that it is neither possible to effect a major change in culture without changing the organisation structure, nor is it possible to make major changes to the organisation structure without having an impact on the culture.

IMPACT OF CULTURE ON MANAGEMENT DEVELOPMENT

There is a clear relationship between an organisation's culture and its approach to management development. The link between the traditional banking and insurance cultures and generic-skills-training-based development is very strong.

Culture can be very effectively transmitted through the development process. In times when changes are needed, this transferrence of values can become a hinderance as well as a help.

Jack Rutley, of the Nationwide, illustrated the problems of 'cultural interference' in his comments about managers' resistance to change. The culture of Nationwide had a significant impact on their development programme. As a result some resistance to change resulted from managers being 'moulded' to a model perceived as relevant to the organisation's requirements. As the organisation's needs changed and a new culture (or at least modified one) emerged, the 'model' underpinning development shifted. In practice a number of managers were resistant to this change and it was (and still is) difficult to 'break the mould'.

In many situations the culture and values of an organisation have a far greater impact on the behaviour of managers than development activities. It is necessary to ensure that development is planned in a way that takes account of the organisation's culture. Brian Chandler of Arthur Young provided a good illustration of the restraining influence of value systems, and ways in which development may be achieved, and skills developed, which are not supported or encouraged in the main business culture.

In order for the example to be able to make its point it is necessary to briefly define some of the key elements in the make-up of the culture of a large accounting firm, such as Arthur Young. The culture throughout the organisation tends to be dominated by that of the core business, which is the audit practice. This is a conservative and cautious culture where procedures, facts and accuracy are dominant values. The focus is technical, rather than commercial. Yet the firms are increasingly moving into the provision of services which are less precise and more commercially focused. Individuals working in the newer areas will have often been trained, and acquired their qualifications, under the influence of the audit culture. A significant challenge, clearly perceived by Brian Chandler, is that of developing commercial awareness and flair in managers, so that the newer business areas may grow successfully.

The case quoted by Brian Chandler relates to a young manager, who was perceived as a high flier with partnership potential. He was sent to one of the firm's Canadian offices – a move designed to broaden his experience as part of the development process. When he returned to the UK there was no evidence of his having acquired a broader outlook.

After returning to the UK he was seconded to a government project, which involved providing help and guidance to small business. During this period, in working with the businesses, he was exposed to a wide range of cultures, but ones with a generally commercial and entrepreneurial focus. The change in his attitude at this time was marked; he had 'discovered business', and could not wait to convert everyone else to his view!

On completion of the secondment he was made a partner in a provincial office. His brief was to develop the office business. Capitalising on the experience and changed views obtained during the secondment he made a success of the job and the business has grown significantly.

The message here is clear. If change in style and approach is required, the development planning must make provision for exposure to a culture supportive of the desired approach to business, and associated skills and attitudes.

Although this case illustrates a successful way of achieving a development goal, Brian Chandler is by no means satisfied. The new partner is now once again exposed to the audit culture. In some situations there are signs of the 'old' culture influencing his behaviour and decisions. In the opinion of Brian Chandler, the impact of the audit culture will only lessen when the top management of the partnership includes non-audit partners.

PRESSURES FOR CHANGE

The culture of an organisation will only, in the long term, be sustainable if it is contributing to the growth and success of the business.

The 'traditional' banking and insurance cultures have survived whilst these organisations have enjoyed profitable and sustained growth. The greatest pressure to change, or modify, an organisation's culture and value systems will often come from changes in the external environment.

The nature and extent of changes currently taking place in the financial sector are inevitably going to lead to changes in the culture in those organisations which will survive and grow. The culture which will emerge must be derived from the overall business needs and strategy and this strategy must be clearly understood throughout the organisation in order that an appropriate culture might be established.

This relationship was clearly illustrated by John Horner of Lombard Continental:

At Lombard Continental the management philosophy and culture is derived from a clear understanding of our business strategy. This strategy is, in simple terms, one of going for profitable expansion based upon sound underwriting. It is a strategy that has proven successful, with the company making underwriting profits in all, but one, classes of business at a time when the market 'norm' has been one of underwriting losses.

As a result of a clear and successful strategy, we have a culture which is characterised by technical excellence being achieved and rewarded; a focus on quality and responsiveness of service (as we will not 'play with rates' to acquire business); careful attention to costs and a high level of commitment to the company and its continued success.

Commitment and enthusiasm with minimal bureaucracy, delegation of responsibility and accountability for results with clearly linked rewards have been policies sponsored by the General Manager. He has recognised that his style is suited to growing a small company and, more importantly, that the way in which the organisation operates must change now that we are on course for further, but less dramatic growth. People will follow the style and lead because results have been achieved. In four years the company has gone from a £1 million loss to a £1 million profit; premium growth has been in excess of 200 per cent with expense ratios generally reducing slightly year by year. In my view these achievements are attributable to the culture developed and successfully propagated at an early stage.

In the larger organisations in the sector the need for change in the culture and value systems is often recognised. However, due to the size of the organisation and the long-established culture, bringing about change can be difficult. External pressures and the force of circumstances can ease the path to change.

In the opinion of many, the changes in the environment will bring about changes in products and ways of operating that will result in a change in culture, without any planned intervention. The challenge to organisations is to manage this change and ensure that it is positively used, rather than letting it occur as a result of force of circumstances.

Jack Rutley of Nationwide has already observed changes occurring in the culture there:

Growth and diversification is giving rise to a need for a change in culture. There already has been a shift away from the traditional 'family' culture and towards a more business related and commercial one.

The impact on the organisation of this, and other changes, is currently only appreciated by a few of the most senior managers. This understanding must become more widespread amongst management, and the consequences planned for and managed.

Peter Rowe, of Lloyds Bank, sees a distinct shift in culture likely to occur as a result of external changes:

Management will become more clinical and competitive. This could affect attitudes to employment and represents a significant shift in the bank's culture. This shift may not be welcomed by many, but it is both essential, and inevitable, in responding to market changes.

Throughout the sector organisations are shifting to a customer orientation. This shift in business focus will inevitably lead to a change in values in many organisations, with customer service becoming a critical value.

INTEGRATION OF DIFFERING CULTURES

The trend towards extending the range of services provided is one of the dominant features in the financial sector.

Introduction of new types of product or service will, almost inevitably, bring with it the introduction of a culture which differs, to a greater or lesser extent, from that which dominates the 'core' business.

The impact and challenge of introducing new services is most readily apparent in those organisations formed as a result of merging banking, stockbroking and jobbing companies in order to effectively compete in the market after 'Big Bang'.

However, the need to deal with differing cultures will also arise in organisations where diversification is to be achieved by either importing new specialists, or redirecting existing skills to deal in new markets.

Thus, many companies in the sector will be faced with a 'multi cultural' organisation. Effective management of this change, and integration of differing cultures, will present a major challenge. The challenge will have to be met in order for organisations to succeed in the changed environment.

Integration of diverse cultures will need to be managed. If it is not, then either a new, and perhaps inappropriate, culture may supplant the core culture. Alternatively, cultural anarchy may result which would impair the cohesive direction of the organisation. The third possibility is that the 'core' culture is imposed on all new business units. The consequence of this could well be that the constraints of the 'core' business also become those of the new business area.

Melvyn Howell, of Midland Bank, provided a good example of the way in which differing market needs can lead to a requirement for differing elements, in cultures and values, emerging in divisions (or units) within the 'core' business of the organisation:

The pressures of differing corporate and retail customer requirements are being felt, and give rise to differing standards or values.

Retail business requires greater product stability; strong shared values in all locations (most importantly, standards of customer service); common approaches to marketing and common image and premises (in terms of layout and standard).

On the other hand, corporate business requires a greater individuality; lower product standardisation; a sharper results and commercial focus tailored to individual needs. Responding to these different needs will lead to the evolution of different cultures. However, both must be managed and integrated into the overall corporate culture.

The main challenge of integrating diverse cultures seems to lay in achieving the balance between allowing the different cultures freedom to apply in the different units of the business, and achieving acceptance of, and commitment to, the overall corporate culture necessary to support cohesive development of the company (or group).

Jeffrey Hernu, of Barclays de Zoette Wedd, is faced with the integration of organisations with significantly different cultures; ranging from that of a merchant banking subsidiary of a UK clearing bank through to that of a firm of stockjobbers.

In his view it is important to identify a range of core policies which will be common throughout the merged organisation and develop, and gain acceptance of, these as a platform for the development of an overall corporate culture and value system. Jeffrey Hernu sees the key policy areas as being:

● Performance appraisal
● Planning and budgeting
● People management
● Succession and manpower planning

Each constituent part of the organisation needs to understand, and support, the corporate needs in these areas. In turn their needs for variation and other specific policies applied at a separate business unit level will be recognised.

This balance is a difficult one to achieve in practice. There can be no hard and fast rules beyond that of recognising the need and working to accommodate it, within the limitations and constraints of the company and its business.

Harry Broomhead, of the Royal Insurance Group, describes their business as having moved sharply to decentralised and relatively autonomous operating companies. The Royal recognised the importance of culture and that with increased autonomy there could well be a divergence of cultures. They recognise the need for divergence in many aspects, but want it to be managed within the framework of overall group values.

Harry Broomhead describes the situation, and Royal's solution, as follows:

> At the Royal we clearly recognise the importance of culture. We are actively developing decentralised and autonomous operations which are supported by group values. In essence this is being achieved by –
>
> - The Group defining the 'what' and standards, or expectations of the operating companies, and
> - The operating companies determining the 'how'.
>
> Basically, in this way, we are establishing areas of influence in which Group and operating company cultures and values may be dominant.

CHANGES NEEDED

In a large number of organisations in the financial sector (and particularly those with a traditional culture) there is a growing recognition of the need to change the culture and value systems.

In many organisations there are different, and specific, changes identified as being necessary. It is, however, possible to identify some changes which are common:

● *Change in management style*

The increasing emphasis on flexibility and responsiveness to customer and market needs will give rise to a need for a change in management style. This will entail a move from a directive, and controlling, style to one where managers are more involved in listening, guiding and facilitating. This change will be particularly important in situations in which managers become involved in managing new specialists brought into the organisation. It will need to be a top down change in style.

● *Greater devolution of responsibility*

There will be a need to move real decision-making closer to the customer, or the market. This will require greater delegation of responsibility and authority.

● *Increasing focus on results*

Attention will need to switch from processes to results. Individuals will need to be targeted to meet objectives, but given the freedom to meet them in the manner that they feel to be best. There will be a move to the manager defining what has to be achieved, and the subordinate determining how it will be achieved. This change will certainly carry with it associated changes in appraisal and reward practices.

● *Move to 'separate business unit' cultures*

Overall, common cultures and value systems covering the whole organisation will not be sustainable as businesses diversify. There will need to be an acceptance that differing cultures and values will emerge in separate business units, whether they are set up as separate companies or divisions within a single company. The need for recognition of this is evident even in 'core' business areas. For example, in a clearing bank the business areas covering electronic banking, or credit cards, do not fit within the 'traditional' retail branch banking culture.

● *End to 'job for life' culture*

Probably one of the most difficult changes to make will be the shift away from the 'job for life' or 'cradle to grave' philosophy. Changes in the market are so dramatic, and rapid, that organisations will have to quickly recognise the need for new skills, and the existence of redundant ones. Dealing with this may well entail bringing in specialists for specific purposes, and not necessarily with a view to their having a full-term career with the organisation. The relatively slow, but continually progressive, approach to career development and the 'grow our own' philosophy, associated with this culture, will have to change. Market conditions will lead to a need to recognise differing 'tiers' of development, and to bring an end to the 'general's baton' philosophy. Development planning will have to become much sharper, and more linked to business realities.

● *Commitment to team work*

Ambiguity and complexity in the environment will militate against the continuation of clearly delineated areas of responsibility.

Reporting relationships and responsibilities will need to become more flexible. Problems and decisions will become more complex and require a mix of skills to solve them.

All of this points to a need to place greater emphasis on team-building and team-work. The importance to team-working, as a strand in the value system, will be underpinned by the need for flexibility, which will result in formation of different teams to deal with different problems and issues. The team-work cultural shift will be tied in with fluidity and changing team composition, rather than an alternative approach to managing fixed groupings of people.

This change may be particularly difficult to affect in an organisation highly focused on individual performance. Malcolm Parker, of Citicorp Investment Bank, sees the need for this change, and the associated problems.

> Citicorp's culture is a strong one, favouring individualists and entrepreneurs. Different people are used at different times to achieve different ends. Within the culture, we will need to develop a commitment to team-work. In order to effect such a change it will be necessary to support the intention with changes to the recognition and reward structure.

EFFECTING CHANGE IN CULTURE

While there is a wide recognition of the need for changes in culture, there is general agreement that bringing about the change is difficult. That some changes are inevitably going to occur raises the problems of managing the change outlined above. Effecting and managing culture change are two issues that need to be addressed in any management development strategy.

The ways in which changes, where seen as necessary, are being effected in the financial sector may be summarised as follows:

Evolution or incremental

In many organisations, change in culture is occurring without any recognition, or consideration, of its implications. However, in a number of organisations this evolutionary change is being recognised and managed. Incremental change is being reinforced through changes to systems impacting on people (for example, appraisal systems), and through the management development process. In particular, the messages underpinning the change are being disseminated and reinforced through the training and education process.

Organisations, such as the Royal Insurance Group and the Legal and General, have successfully effected significant shifts in their culture and value systems by planning and managing incremental change. In some cases the change has evolved over a good many years, and is expected to evolve further.

The active management of evolutionary change frequently involves taking the opportunity presented by a change in the external environment, and using this to effect a needed shift in the culture. Effective management of evolutionary change, is very significantly, business driven.

Revolution

Evolution of culture takes time. Organisations in the financial sector with a strong 'traditional' culture, faced with a very different market, may not have time to adopt an evolutionary approach.

Change in culture may have to be achieved by significant shifts in emphasis within the systems impacting on people.

Greater devolution of authority and accountability, and shifts to 'separate business unit' structures, will have to happen over a relatively short period of time. Such changes will need to be supported by changes in reward and appraisal systems as well as by training and education programmes.

Revolutionary change is unsettling. To be effectively implemented, and managed, it is necessary to communicate clearly the reasons for, and direction of, the change.

The onus will be on the board to define and communicate clearly the values necessary for survival and growth of the organisation. Communication must clearly define the business strategy and the values, which are necessary to execute that strategy, and achieve the business goals. Resources need to be made available to provide the support which will be necessary to implement the required changes.

'Seeding'

In organisations where there is either a failure to recognise the need for change in culture and values, or an absence of a structure to effectively identify and manage change, results can be achieved by 'seeding' the organisation with people attuned to the problems and needs. This approach is one used by Brian Chandler of Arthur Young:

> The structure and nature of Arthur Young does not lend itself to highly centralised management development. Its structure, and the strength of the audit culture, militate against rapid planned change in values, styles and climate. In this environment the only effective strategy is a guerrilla one. Key people, open to change, are identified and then developed by exposure to new ideas and thinking.
>
> They are nurtured. A relationship is developed which allows me to counsel and coach them in the application of new thinking to their job. These people are 'seeded' in the different units and, periodically, brought together (often under the guise of a training programme) to obtain reinforcement for their new thinking and approaches to business.
>
> These 'seeds' will spread change. They will influence others in their business units. If they have been well chosen they will be successful in terms of results and promotion. In this way they will move up in the organisation and provide a channel for developing more rapid and widespread change. At the same time their style, values and approaches to business will be seen to be successful and be imitated by others.
>
> This is a long-term strategy and requires a regular flow of 'seeds'. However, we are seeing results and with these results it becomes easier to win over and develop new 'seeds' and to develop 'change cells' in the firm.

In a less strategically planned way other organisations use a 'seeding' approach to effecting change. Commonly this takes the form of sending selected managers on external courses, where it is anticipated that they will acquire new ideas which they will then import into the organisation.

PRESERVING CURRENT BENEFITS AND DEVELOPING A POSITIVE CLIMATE

Any process of change carries with it the danger of losing the positive benefits associated with the original position. This is particularly so in relation to changes in culture and value systems.

Many of the cultures identified as needing to change, in order to enable organisations to respond to the changed environment, carry positive benefits as well as having disadvantages.

It is important that care is taken in the direction and management of change, not to lose relevant benefits from the existing culture. Positive features should be built on, not destroyed. For example, in Skandinaviska Enskilda Banken in Sweden there has been a strong culture of 'growing their own' management. This has carried on with the advantage of creating a climate of loyalty and continuity. However, the pressures of change in the external environment have highlighted weaknesses. The nature of the market is one requiring increased commercialism and business flair. The 'grow our own' philosophy has produced managers with a relatively narrow outlook and experience, who are not fully able to meet the changing needs of the market. An abandonment of the 'grow our own' philosophy and extensive use of external recruitment would enable the drawbacks of the current value to be overcome. However, it would also result in a loss of its benefits.

They have faced this issue and are modifying their philosophy to meet immediate short-term needs (that is, recruiting where essential for key positions) and implementing training programmes to broaden the outlook and commercial awareness of the managers in the medium term. The changes are not revolutionary. However, they are felt to be critical, and thus are supported by a clear communication of their nature and aims, and the business needs driving them.

Change is uncomfortable; effecting and managing it is far easier if the current culture, and value systems, engender a positive climate.

There are many views on what makes for a positive working climate. Below are the elements, of such a climate, on which there is certainly a good deal of agreement in the financial sector:

● Jobs are structured and managed in such a way that employees feel that they, and their talents, are needed by the organisation. This implies a delegation of responsibility and accountability. This is a feature that the move towards a 'separate business unit' organisation will reinforce.

● Open communication exists at all levels. It is important that good two-way communication channels exist and are actively used. In operational terms it is important that managers and their people have regular discussions on work and business requirements, as well as personal performance.

● Fair reward for performance. Reward here should be seen in broad terms. Not only should financial rewards reflect contribution and performance, but also the promotion and development systems should reflect the value that performance is recognised and rewarded. Equally, on a day-to-day basis, management style should be such that time is taken to praise as well as to guide, correct and criticise.

● A clear understanding of business strategy, goals and organisation is developed. All employees should be able to see what is happening in the organisation, in the context of an overall business strategy clearly related to the requirements of the market.

There are certainly other elements which could be identified. However, the above 'core' elements appear to be the most significant. Although many senior managers would accept the importance of these key elements, the practical development of a positive climate is highly dependant upon their perceived commitment to the values identified. This commitment requires more than words. Dr Guth summarised the importance of *real* commitment in his address at the International Conference on Bank Training in March 1986:

There is one thing I would like to emphasise: the decisive importance of the example set by senior management for the general climate in the company and thus for the motivation of its staff. Their conduct and their style influence the climate throughout the entire organisation. In the long run every company, every bank can only be as good as its top management.

CULTURE AND MANAGEMENT DEVELOPMENT STRATEGY

Throughout this chapter the links between an organisation's culture and value systems and management development processes have been considered.

In planning a management development strategy it is important to take full account of culture. Having identified future skill, performance and organisational requirements for the business overall, and its separate business units, there is a need to think about the cultures necessary to underpin the needs. Plans may then be evolved to bring about an appropriate change in culture as a part of overall development planning. To develop the linkage in practice, and to bring about the desired changes in culture, requires the following stages to be undertaken:

– *Identify the current culture*

Obtain people's perceptions. Review the picture that emerges of both the formal and informal elements of the current culture, both in relation to the overall organisation and the individual business units.

– *Match culture to markets*

Identify the most appropriate internal culture in the separate business units to match and support the external environment in which they will be operating (for example, what type of internal environment will be needed to operate in the highly entrepreneurial capital markets business).

– *Establish needs for organisation change*

Identify the type of organisation structure which will be necessary to accommodate required changes in culture (for example, a matrix organisation may be more appropriate than a traditional hierarchy in a competitive sales and marketing climate).

– *People/job matches*

Having identified the required culture and organisation structure to meet future needs, it is necessary to review the match between people and jobs. It may well be necessary to change people/job matches in order to either achieve, or manage, the required change in culture.

Going through this process will result in the formation of a management development strategy which is integrated with the culture in a way which will help ensure its contribution to the current and future needs of the business.

SUMMARY

The important interdependency of management development and organisational culture and values has, hopefully, been made clear in this chapter.

Whilst it is difficult to generalise about cultures it is possible to identify a number of common cultures in the financial sector. These are:

- Those found in the larger banks and insurers. This culture is seen as the 'traditional' one in this sector and is characterised by:

  - 'job for life' philosophy
  - 'grow our own' approach to development
  - generous remuneration
  - centralised decision-making
  - over-recruitment and underutilisation of skills and talent
  - caring and often 'paternalistic' attitude towards employees
  - focus on processes and not on results

- Those found in the more dynamic organisations, which have a successful track record and have undergone significant growth. These are characterised by:

  - focus on results and not processes
  - business-driven
  - high delegation of responsibility and accountability
  - willingness to take risks is encouraged and mistakes are tolerated

These two cultures tend to represent the extremes of a continuum. Market changes are tending to move 'traditional' cultures along the spectrum towards the results-driven ones.

Building societies have a rather unusual culture, due to their origins. These cultures tend to be strongly influenced by social objectives. Many societies feel that adherence to their value systems will provide a competitive edge in the changing markets. Others feel that they must evolve a more commercially directed culture in order to survive.

The culture of organisations in the financial sector is frequently reflected in the way in which they are structured. 'Traditional' businesses tend to have a highly centralised structure, whilst the results-driven businesses are increasingly devolving authority to separate business units, which enjoy a high degree of autonomy within the overall structure.

An organisation's culture can effectively be disseminated and supported by the management development processes. Equally, unless its significance is recognised, it can act as a barrier to the changes which the development process is trying to achieve. Culture and value systems can have a far greater impact on the behaviour of managers than can development activities. It is essential that management development planning takes account of cultural factors. Changing the behaviour of managers to meet new business needs may necessitate exposing them to different, and varied, cultures and value systems.

Changes in the financial sector environment are creating pressures on many organisations which will result in a change in culture and style. The general shift to a customer orientation, and the need to be more responsive to changes in markets, will have a major impact on cultures in many businesses.

The expansion in range of services whether achieved by merger, acquisition, recruitment or reorganisation, will inevitably give rise to the evolution of differing cultures. It will be essential to manage the integration of these cultures in the organisation. The major challenge in dealing with integration will be achieving a balance between gaining commitment to corporate values and allowing business units freedom to develop their own appropriate and relevant values.

The major changes in culture and values identified as being necessary to meet the demands of a changing environment are:

● Changing management style towards a more supportive and facilitating, and less directive, one
● Greater devolution of responsibility
● Increasing focus on results and rewarding achievement
● Evolution of separate business-unit cultures
● Ending the 'job for life' culture
● Commitment to team-working

Approaches to bringing about change in culture were seen as falling into the following categories:

● Evolutionary or incremental
● Revolutionary
● 'Seeding' the organisation with individuals committed to change.

Faced with the need to change, it is important not to lose the positive attributes of the existing culture.

In any culture which is successful there appear to be the following ingredients which promote a positive environment:

- All employees feel their skills are needed and valued
- Open communication at all levels
- Fair reward for performance
- A clear understanding of the business strategy and goals is widely shared

In planning a management development strategy it is essential that both existing and required cultures are taken into account. To do this the key steps are:

- Clearly identify the current culture
- Match the culture to the needs of the markets
- Establish requirements for change
- Match people, jobs and culture in the most effective way

A management development strategy which takes full account of the role and impact of culture and value systems will be successful in contributing to the survival and growth of an organisation.

6 Moving on a Broad Front

Previous chapters have portrayed a climate of far-reaching and, in many instances, fundamental change. Change is taking place in the business environment which is driving changes in organisation, culture, the nature of managerial jobs and perceptions and expectations of the management development process.

To meet these changed needs and expectations it is necessary to formulate cohesive management development strategy, related to the current and future goals of the business. Such a strategy must be designed to make a significant contribution to the achievement of these business goals.

In this chapter the main considerations which need to be taken into account in the formulation of an effective management development strategy are reviewed. In addition a framework for planning a management development strategy is presented.

LINKING MANAGEMENT DEVELOPMENT TO THE BUSINESS STRATEGY

Within the financial sector there is a growing recognition that management development should be business driven, rather than based upon academic models of general management skills. In earlier chapters the need for management development to be integrated with the business planning processes was highlighted.

If this move to business-driven management development is to be realised, it is essential that formulation of the management development strategy begins with the establishment of a clear understanding of the overall business strategy.

The time frame of the management development strategy needs to match that of the overall corporate one. The increasingly tentative nature of business planning in the current volatile environment means that the management development strategy will have to retain a degree of flexibility, to underpin responses to changing market conditions.

The strategic business plan will provide a framework for the development strategy. Emerging from this plan will be clear indications of the skills and talents which will be required; the way in which the organisation is likely to be structured and the core business values. To be really effective, the management development planning process should interact with the corporate planning process. At the minimum it should be responsive to the requirements of the corporate strategy. However, it should be providing input to the formulation of such strategy. The development process, and issues, may make available new options and resources to be taken into account in the corporate strategy. Equally achievement of certain corporate aims may be constrained by development issues. This two-way process will lead to both a more realistic corporate strategy, and a clear framework for a strongly business-driven management development strategy.

GAINING SUPPORT FOR, AND COMMITMENT TO, THE MANAGEMENT DEVELOPMENT STRATEGY

In many organisations the initiatives for management development are now being seen coming from the very top of the company. Senior management are beginning to see management development as being essential to the survival and growth of the business.

Illustrative of this trend is the way in which the Nationwide Building Society has changed the way in which management development is organised. Jack Rutley described the change:

> The recognition of the need for, and drive to introduce, a cohesive management development strategy has been initiated by the chief executive. To bring about the change, he required the establishment of a separate management development function.
>
> Management development, as a function, reports to an operational general manager. The aim of this is to change line management perceptions of the function from that of a service one to that of an operational one. Management development is seen as being field oriented rather than as part of the head office administration.

Without the support and commitment of senior and line managers, the management development process will be constrained from contributing to business performance. It will remain perceived as a peripheral activity.

There is wide recognition of the need to obtain management

support and commitment. However, it is equally recognised that securing such support and commitment can be difficult; it requires a major change in managerial perceptions being effected. Harry Broomhead, of the Royal Insurance Group, summarised the need and the problems facing personnel management both at Group level and at operating company level:

> We are fortunate in that the Chief Executive of the Group has made the subject of management succession and development and manpower planning priority areas – as they are in the minds of the Chief Executives of each of the operating companies.
>
> However, it is still essential to main the support and commitment of management down the line to management development. Whilst education and communication clearly play an important part in securing commitment to management development, relevance and involvement are most important factors in gaining managements' support.

If the management development strategy and processes are clearly geared to business needs, then management are likely to provide the support required. If line managers have been involved with, and had an input to, the management development strategy, a high level of support is likely to be obtained. If the involvement continues in implementing the strategy, and if the strategy is suitably flexible to meet changing market needs, the line managers are likely to remain committed and supportive.

ORGANISATION STRUCTURE

The way in which the organisation is structured is a factor which needs to be taken into account in formulating a management development strategy. The strategy may be constrained by an existing structure, or may be required to provide support for evolving new structures. In some situations modification of the organisation structure may be a pre-requisite for achieving development goals.

Earlier chapters have pointed to the requirement to evolve differing structures to deal with the diverse range of products and markets. These differing organisation structures are likely to give rise to needs for differing management development strategies. Melvyn Howell of Midland Bank sees the evolution of differing strategies, to meet a range of needs, as being a major management development issue.

There is a need for differentiated management development and career structures to match the growth of differentiated business needs and organisation structures.

The differentiated model of development will give rise to recognition of differing knowledge and skill requirements, differing professional qualifications and career, and job, structures in the separate business units.

But despite the critical emphasis on achieving successful 'people performance' in the separate business units, the core development process must support the needs of running the organisation as a whole.

The need for a differentiated management development strategy was also seen as important by Peter Rowe of Lloyds Bank. He sees the movement to separate business units as inevitable. However, differentiated development strategies, in his view, will only be viable if the separate business units are large enough to offer some form of career structure within each of them. The development strategy will also need to address the development of corporate resources in a differentiated organisation. Peter Rowe sees this as leading to the development of a 'corporate resource'. People in this group would undergo a development process which entails crossing separate business unit boundaries, and provides a basis for developing the skills and experience necessary for the overall management of the bank in the future.

Jeffrey Hernu, of Barclays de Zoette Wedd, sees that companies in the financial sector are increasingly likely to have four major components in their structure. He sees these as being:

● *'Factory'*

The processing and basic administration of the business will become highly automated and increasingly 'deskilled'. This will result in the operations being supported by 'factories' processing paper and documents.

● *Operational management*

Those responsible for obtaining and managing business in the business units.

● *Corporate management*

Those responsible for planning for and managing the organisation as a whole.

● *'High flyer, skilled specialists'*

As specialists, this group will often have a high mobility, moving in and out of the bank and looking for high rewards rather than commitment and development.

Management development strategy will clearly be influenced by the way in which these elements are combined in the organisation; the degree to which mobility between the elements will be necessary and the degree of autonomy devolved upon operational management.

The separate business unit trend in organisation structure is clearly going to have an important impact on management development strategy. The requirement to meet the current and future needs of the business units will become clear. However, it will be important for the strategy to address the issue of developing future corporate management, and meshing this with the separate business unit requirements.

Superimposed on the above organisational considerations is likely to be a change in the hierarchical structure of organisations in the financial sector. With market and product changes it is likely that organisations will become flatter.

This 'flattening' of organisations will also be accompanied by changes in skill mixes and requirements. Increasing use of technology will eliminate many of the basic and routine jobs. With this will emerge a reduced requirement for supervisory skills, which have traditionally been associated with the management of large numbers of people doing basic and routine tasks.

For many companies this change will eliminate a number of steps in development paths. There will no longer be the possibility of incremental movement through the range of supervisory positions into the managerial structure. In turn, in the managerial structure, there are likely to be fewer levels, which again will make incremental career movement difficult to use as part of the development strategy.

The implication of these changes in structure are two-fold. First, development strategy will have to be geared to providing people with managerial skills without the support of incremental job experience. Secondly, the flatter structures will reduce the number of openings for promotion. This will advance in time the problems of career plateaux. Plateauing is already a fairly common problem, particularly as many development programmes raise expectations of continued upward movement. As organisations change in structure these career plateaux may be reached at a far earlier stage.

Unless the management development strategy effectively changes aspirations away from those of continued upward mobility, it is likely that organisations will be faced with morale problems and frustration amongst younger managers. It is these managers whose support and commitment will be required, and who will need to be flexible and adaptable to help the organisation survive and grow.

BUSINESS AND PRODUCT LIFE CYCLES

In planning a management development strategy it is necessary to take account of the business and product life cycles impacting on the business.

Current market conditions are leading to increasingly short product life cycles. If product grouping is the base for organisational identification of separate business units, the management development strategy will have to take full account of the speed with which the product life cycle may be completed. The likely organisational changes which will result, as one product enters a mature or declining phase and another enters the growth phase, will also have to be considered.

Consideration of business life cycles will impact on skill requirements, operational climate, and reward systems which need to be addressed by the management development strategy. As business areas are seen as having different life cycles they will have different organisational and managerial requirements. For example, emerging business units (such as capital markets businesses) will require entrepreneurial skills and a climate of high freedom of action, focus on results and strong performance reward systems. On the other hand a mature business (such as retail banking) will require managerial skills more directed towards problem solving and the application of managerial 'techniques', in an environment which is structured and controlled.

CAREER PATHS AND CAREER CYCLES

Current views and practice in relation to management development in the financial sector are influenced by the 'career for life' philosophy. There is a general expectation that a person joining an organisation will stay with that organisation until they retire.

The emergence of highly-mobile specialists has begun to influence this 'career for life' perception. In some areas there is a recognition that the specialists have a fairly short life cycle. For example, foreign exchange dealers are widely believed to have a working life of some 10 to 20 years. Beyond this there is a feeling that the stresses and pressures of the job are such as to lead to some form of 'burn out'. When this perception emerges, the approach to reward and development changes significantly. High rewards over a relatively short career life, with no commitment to continuing development at the end of that period, is a common model for foreign exchange dealers.

In addition to changes in an organisation's thinking, it is clear that individuals are developing new perceptions in relation to their own careers. The acceptance that a career is characterised by pressure for regular promotion through to retirement is declining. Increasingly, 'quality of life' is becoming a significant factor in individual's decisions on career aspirations. Companies which have traditionally moved people functionally and geographically every few years are finding, increasingly, that employees are declining geographic moves on the grounds that the impact on the family's quality of life is unacceptable.

There is an increasing recognition that, for many jobs and many individuals, a shorter working life is inevitable. The main barrier to this change happening quickly is the provision of pensions. Loss of pension rights on job change, or early retirement, can tend to be punitive. This 'locks' many people into continuing employment with the same employer. It is likely that this constraint will be removed in the not too distant future, given a legislative climate of encouraging portability and individual ownership of pensions.

Thinking on the length of careers, and changing individual career perceptions and aspirations is, then, one aspect of changing career paths in financial sector organisations. The other aspect relates to the business and the organisation structures. Earlier in this chapter the need to consider organisation structure in development strategy was highlighted.

With this change in structure needs to come a change in thinking on career paths and recruitment policy.

Perhaps the most fundamental change is in the recognition of the need for tiered career paths, and thus tiered recruitment.

A common view is that there will be one level, or tier, of recruitment associated with the 'paper factory' or 'shop floor' jobs. All recruitment will no longer be based on the view that every job gives access to a career path to the top. Basic level recruitment will move more towards recruitment to perform specific jobs, rather than to embark on a career path. The reward structure for these jobs will be on a 'rate for the job' basis. A move to acceptance of this tier in recruitment and career structure will have a major impact on the management development strategy. Planning for this tier of the business is likely to relate to relatively short career paths leading, perhaps, to a supervisory role. However, such a change will have implications in terms of the culture and values predominant in this part of organisations; and the managerial style and skills required for the effective management of these functions.

In making such a change there is a widespread view that paths should be left open for talented individuals to be able to cross over into other career structures.

Career structures and life cycles in the separate business units are expected to vary significantly, with high speed development and potential early 'burn out' in the highly entrepreneurial units; and a pattern closer to the traditional one in the more mature core business units. As the move to separate business units accelerates it is anticipated that authority for recruitment and career development policies will also be devolved.

The focus of career planning and development in the business units will be on the business, continuity and succession needs of those units. This focus is 'parochial' and does not take account of the needs for the development of corporate management. Increasingly a view is developing that corporate management needs may be best met by a tier of recruits who are viewed as a corporate resource. These people will have their development managed corporately, although they will spend planned periods of time in the separate business units. It is likely that the career cycle of those in corporate positions will be longer than that of many in the separate business units. They will, however, need to be developed to take on real managerial accountability at a relatively early stage in their careers.

Overall, there is a realisation that movement between the separate business unit management and corporate management must be kept open. Paths will be needed to enable people to move from a corporate resource development group into a career in a business unit, and vice versa.

In some organisations there is a feeling that corporate, or group, needs may be met without recourse to a separate tier of recruitment and career path. In these organisations the development strategy is highly geared to increasing the breadth and commercial awareness of managers in the separate business units. Those managers who develop and perform effectively in these units are seen as a 'resource' which may readily be called on to fill a corporate, or group, succession requirement. Covering for the movement of such people into a central management role is seen as part of the unit management's role, in developing their own succession and continuity plans.

Detailed career paths planning at an individual level is felt to be unnecessary by a number of organisations, if the right climate is created. Peter Birch of Abbey National holds the view that:

> People tend to sort out their own level in career terms. We need to provide the support for this individual decision-making through our management development and appraisal programmes.

This is a view supported by David Woodward of Scandinavian Bank who observes that:

> In general we find that people do tend to demonstrate a degree of self-selection. Those with further career aspirations do push for their own development. We must ensure that we provide the right climate and support for these people.

In looking at career paths in terms of their relationship to management development strategy, it is important to recognise a diversity of career options. Too often the wrong people have been placed in management jobs, as there has been a single growth or career path in the organisation. A recognition of the need for technical career paths, as well as managerial ones, is growing in many companies.

Harry Broomhead of the Royal Insurance Group has clearly identified two major considerations in this technical/managerial balance. First, there is the danger that exposure in technical areas (a necessary part of development) can adversely affect subsequent development of managerial skills and thinking:

> People of high potential, entering technical jobs, have to be watched to ensure that the focus does not remain too narrow for too long. Early action is necessary to broaden their horizons and provide an early managerial learning input.

The second consideration relates to the provision of real career options. Harry Broomhead sees a need for at least three routes in any of the business units. He sees these as being:

- *Managerial route* – Movement from the specialist technical area into broader, and more commercially-based, managerial roles; and then (for some) to general management roles.

- *Technical, vertical route* – This is a path involving development, in a hierarchical sense, in a technical function. In essence it involves growth into technically-based supervisory and managerial jobs.

- *Technical, horizontal route* – A path allowing for growth as a specialist, and broadening of technical experience, through expanded responsibilities and/or project exposure.

What is clear from the points raised in relation to career paths is that their diversity is growing and life cycle shortening. Effective planning of management development strategy requires that existing paths are reviewed, their implications considered, and that new options are both anticipated and indeed promoted, in the strategy.

IMPACT OF CULTURE AND PRESENT DEVELOPMENT PROCESSES

The interrelationship between organisational culture and the development process has been examined in the previous chapter. In planning a management development strategy it is essential to consider both the current culture and future likely, or desired, ones.

It is also important to consider how the past and current development processes have shaped the behaviour of managers. Indeed, it is evident that existing managers have a significant impact on the behaviour, and values, of subordinates aspiring to promotion, and of new managers.

Brian Chandler, of Arthur Young, has identified this behaviour-shaping aspect of culture as one of the major barriers to change, unless it is managed and used positively. He refers to the process as 'imprinting'.

The degree to which existing culture, norms, style and methods have been imprinted on managers is a bigger change inhibitor than age of managers.

This often exhibits itself in the frequent tendency for younger managers, who have been through a development programme strong in 'traditional' culture, to be resistant to change, a tendency noted by Jack Rutley of Nationwide Building Society (see Chapter 5).

Brian Chandler sees existing managers as having a key impact as 'imprinters'. This role can be used positively if these managers can be developed to accept the norms of change. The 'seeding' process described in Chapter 5 uses this 'imprinting' role to bring about change in values in the organisation.

In addition to influences within an organisation, values may be 'imprinted' by external development activities. Obtaining professional qualifications provides a good example of this. In an accounting firm the audit culture is strongly supported, and reinforced, by the professional qualification and training process.

Thus, in planning a management development strategy, it is important to consider external influences on development, such as training and education leading to professional and other qualifications, as well as the impact of the internal culture.

Development strategy needs to be designed to affect the organisations younger managers at an early stage, in order to be able to encourage desired values and behaviour before 'imprinting' has made its mark.

The strength of existing culture and value systems needs to be borne in mind when formulating a management development strategy. A strong culture can produce a cohesive and committed organisation. The 'bonding' resulting from such a strong culture can be very valuable in a stable environment. However, when the environment changes it may prove difficult to break, and reform, these strong 'bonds' without weakening the structure. In fact, in an unstable environment, organisations where the 'bonding' is weaker may find it somewhat easier to respond to the pressures of change.

Generally to achieve a dramatic change in an organisation's approach to management development it is necessary to effect a change in culture and values.

SUCCESSION PLANNING

From the strategic business plan and a review of organisation requirements, and current and future career paths, it will be possible to identify major succession needs.

Management development strategy must be clearly directed towards meeting the organisation's succession requirements. In examining succession planning, the identification of the organisation's needs is one element, the others are to look at the 'pool' from which successors will be drawn, and to consider how the process will be managed. The questions and issues that are raised are:

- Who are the 'key players'? It is important that information is available covering their performance, skills, potential and, importantly, their own aspirations. Too frequently succession plans are built on assumptions that all of those with potential wish to continue to progress in the organisation.

- Where are they going, and in what time frame? Identification of career paths for the 'key players', and the likely time to move along those paths, is an important stage in succession planning

- How long to develop them? How long does it take, based upon current practice, to develop the 'key players' to reach the different points on the career paths?

- How much should people be told? Communication plays an important part in an effective management development strategy. Communication of information on succession plans is invariably a sensitive area. In the financial sector it is relatively rare to find organisations prepared to disclose to the 'player' their detailed long-term plans. However, there is a growing realisation that it is important that people should know that they are 'in the running'. An increasing number of companies in the sector are letting people know that they are in the 'pool' from which senior level successors are selected.

Communication should be a two-way process. At most levels open communication should take place, covering both the management's views on career possibilities for individuals, and actively seeking their views on their own development and aspirations.

The communication should be realistic as well as open. It is important for managers to avoid raising unrealistic levels of expectation in their staff. Achieving a balance between openness, without detail, and realism, is difficult. However, the effort is well worth it if a healthy climate for development is to be established.

In addition to the questions raised above, a fundamental consideration arises in connection with succession planning. That is the question of numbers of potential successors to be developed for each position. Companies, whose philosophy is that individuals will push for their own development, usually have a culture which results in sufficient numbers of potential successors emerging.

Other organisations tend to have a range of views on the extent of cover which needs to be developed. At one end of this spectrum of views is the philosophy that a large and competitive 'pool' should be established. In this way they feel that they will be assured of good calibre successors. At the other extreme a 'crowned prince' syndrome emerges with almost one for one cover being developed.

Donald Kirkham, of the Woolwich Equitable Building Society, argues strongly for a middle course:

We need to avoid the danger of creating a pool with too many people with high levels of skill and ambition. Doing this can result in morale problems. It creates a situation which is difficult to manage, and is both expensive and wasteful of resources.

Succession planning requirements play a significant role in the formulation of management development strategy. As with other considerations, the strategy needs to consider both the implications of current practice and the need for change to meet changing business requirements. For example, a highly-mechanistic approach to succession planning may constrain the development of a flexible and adaptable managerial resource. In such a case, management development strategy may require a change in approach to succession planning as one means of facilitating achievement of business and development goals.

JOB PROFILES AND ASSESSMENT

Reviewing succession planning inevitably leads to two further considerations in formulating a management development strategy. These are:

● What will be the requirements and nature of the jobs to be filled?
● How will the 'key players' be spotted, and at what stage?

Chapter 2 highlighted the changing nature of managerial jobs and, due to the volatile environment, the difficulty in arriving at a precise definition of future job requirements. Although it is difficult to produce specific job definitions for future posts, it is important to analyse and profile likely future skill requirements. At the core of an effective management development strategy is the need for a process to match people to jobs, as accurately as possible. Therefore, some form of job profiling, covering both present and future managerial jobs, is necessary to form a basis for the job-matching process.

At the Scandinavian Bank, David Woodward has recognised the need for clear job profiles.

In management development planning it is important to develop clear job profiles. These do not only take the form of job descriptions, but are also expressed in terms of factors critical to the achievement of results.

At the Legal and General there is a move towards developing clear pictures of top job requirements by analysis of critical success factors and behaviour skills. Although this approach overcomes the problems of precise definition of future jobs, it does raise difficulties in terms of identifying who should be responsible for defining the critical success factors. The Scandinavian Bank found that existing job-holders tended to have a limited, and historical, perspective. As a result the critical success factors they identified covered only some 50 per cent of the *real* requirements of the job.

Legal and General is using a group-based specialist management development resource in compiling more comprehensive details of senior jobs in terms of defined skills and behaviour.

The important point about profiling managerial behaviour, characteristics and roles within an organisation is that it provides a highly specific model on which to build a management development strategy. This model is relevant to the business, and its markets, and provides a more focused basis for development than do the generic skills models that are so commonly encountered.

Within the financial sector there is a growing awareness of the need to spot people with potential for development at an early stage. With this awareness has emerged a growing interest in assessment processes and techniques.

In order to achieve optimum people/job-matching, it is essential that good information on individual's performance, skills, interests, aspirations and potential is established and maintained. Thus, in formulating a management development strategy, it is important to consider the adequacy of information held on people, and the processes used for assessing potential.

The use of a skill and critical success factor basis of profiling jobs provides a sound framework for developing assessment processes.

There is a need for regular assessment in order to ensure that the organisation's development needs are properly met. David Woodward, at Scandinavian Bank, identifies effective assessment processes as a key element in their development strategy:

> Once people have been recruited, there is a need for a continuous process of assessment in order to optimise the matching of people to jobs.

It is essential that the assessment criteria are closely tied to the job's profiles and business needs. The Royal Group's devolution of much of the assessment process to the business units recognises this, and enables criteria to be developed to allow for assessment process relevant to the business-unit's markets and needs. Above the business-unit level, the Royal have an assessment process to deal with identification of potential for corporate or Group management.

Effective management development strategy thus needs job profiling and assessment processes at both business-unit and corporate levels. The strategy needs to encompass the facility for differing profiling, assessment processes and criteria to be formulated to meet the operating and developmental requirements of the differing units in the organisation.

A FRAMEWORK FOR PLANNING A MANAGEMENT DEVELOPMENT STRATEGY

Having reviewed the major considerations, which need to be borne in mind in formulating a management development strategy, it is useful to consider a systematic approach to putting the strategy together.

The objective of an effective management development strategy will be to enhance current organisational performance and to ensure future performance and growth.

The planning process to achieve this objective will involve the following elements:

- Organisation analysis
- Manager assessment
- Management development
- Management succession

Organisation analysis

The process of organisational analysis will entail reviewing current, and predicted, business strategies and environments, and, from these, deriving the current and future organisational and manpower requirements.

Manager assessment

Effective planning requires that a clear profile of skills and talent in the organisation is established. This will entail systematically collecting, and reviewing, information on the current and past performance of managers. There will also be a need to obtain a clear picture of the potential of managers for further growth and development.

Management development

Organisational and managerial assessments will result in the identification of current performance gaps, and future skill gaps. Management development programmes will need to be produced for both individuals and groups. These programmes will need to be designed to enhance current performance and to develop skills to meet future requirements.

Management succession

Analysing future needs, and managerial potential, will provide information which will enable succession decisions to be made effectively. The planned approach to management succession will ensure that decisions relating to the movement of people will be clearly understood. In addition the decisions will need to be seen as equitable, logical and beneficial to all concerned.

NEEDS ANALYSIS

The process of needs analysis will entail reviewing many facets of the organisation, in order to establish a clear picture of current and future manpower requirements. This picture will be matched with an analysis of skills and potential. The *gaps* identified in this matching process will be analysed to determine action required in terms of development, training, career planning, education and recruitment.

The key steps in the needs analysis programme will be:

- Analysis of current business plans, group and subsidiary organisation structures.

- Review of future business strategies.

- Identification of future organisation, and key jobs, structures to deal with changes and implement proposed strategies.

- Identification of the extent to which separate business units will emerge; and analysis of the range of organisational and manpower requirements.

- Development of a current managerial skills inventory and review of current performance.

- Analysis of career paths offered in current and future

organisation structures. This analysis will need to take into account the increasing need for cross-functional mobility.

● Development of a profile of potential for current managers.

● Conduct a gap analysis to identify:

- Needs to improve current performance.

- Needs to develop and realise potential.

- Needs for skills which may not be met by internal promotion or transfer.

- Needs for long-term recruitment programmes and career planning.

The needs profile which emerges from this analysis will form the basis on which action plans and programmes will be developed.

Individual, as well as group, development plans will be produced.

SUMMARY

The rapidly changing environment in which financial sector organisations are now operating is giving rise to a range of new pressures. In general the following trends are common:

● Increasing destandardisation of products

● Greater product innovation coupled with shorter product life cycles

● Increasing use of temporary organisation structures to deal with specific problems and issues

● A growing need for people to be able to learn and develop rapidly

A number of major financial sector organisations are currently re-examining their management development strategies and practices to determine how they may accelerate the development of skills to meet the challenges of a changing and uncertain environment.

A further notable trend is that different business areas are seen as having different life cycles, and subsequently different organisational and managerial requirements. Management of such diversity is being achieved through breaking an organisation into separate business units (SBU's). The managerial skills and climate in each unit will largely be determined by its phase in the business life cycle. For example, an emerging business unit, such as capital markets, will require entrepreneurial skills operating in a climate of high freedom of action and strong performance reward systems. On the other hand, a mature business (perhaps retail banking) will require managerial skills more directed towards problem solving and the application of 'management techniques' operating in a more structured and controlled climate.

Against this background the following considerations need to be borne in mind in formulating a management development strategy:

- Different business areas/units will have differing needs and, perhaps, different policies.

- Changing environments will lead to changing internal climates and organisation structures. Thus culture and structure is unlikely to be a constant factor in development planning.

- The need for flexibility and responsiveness will require a broad-based approach to development. For example, changing organisation structure may become a viable development vehicle.

- To develop flexibility it will be necessary to plan for an increasing degree of mobility and cross-function change in development programmes.

- This requirement will need to be reviewed in the light of the organisation's personnel policy. The continuation of a 'grow our own' managers' policy will require development of consistent supportive policies to underpin, and ease, the pressure to change and develop which would be placed on managers.

- There will be a requirement to develop a broad mix of skills and to have a process of effectively matching skills to the needs of different business areas or units.

- Overall, the need for flexibility and the extent and rate of change will require effective communication of policy. Prior to this it will be necessary to involve senior management in the formulation of policy and action plans in order to ensure understanding and secure commitment.

For management development to make a significant contribution to business performance, it is clear that a considerable effort must be directed to the formulation of a business-driven strategy. Many of the considerations in formulating a strategy are wide ranging. It is evident that developing an effective strategy entails management development issues and planning being actively integrated with the organisation's core business planning processes. It is no longer feasible to view management development as a peripheral activity, or one that may take place outside of the real management of the business.

7 Developing Tomorrow's Manager

Having examined the need for a change in management development strategy, and identified possible future directions, it is now useful to look at what is currently happening, in development terms, in the financial sector.

This chapter examines the changes in thinking and practice in the sector. To illustrate both the range of changes, and common threads, the chapter reviews thinking and practice in a range of specific companies; as well as identifying the main common strands in current thinking in the sector.

The companies reviewed are grouped into the three major divisions of banking, insurance and building societies.

BANKING

Midland Bank

Melvyn Howell (Manager, Management Development – Retail Banking Sector) has identified a far-reaching range of changes which need to occur, in his view, if the banks are to address successfully the challenges facing them. He does, however, recognise that in large organisations it is difficult to bring about radical change quickly.

What he sees is an agenda for change which must be carefully examined. The main changes identified as being important to implement are:

- A need to move away from a single, bankwide, career structure to 'multi structures', which cater for both specialists and generalists. This is closely tied to a recognition of the need for the organisation to move to a separate business unit philosophy. Midland are currently making this move to a structure of discrete business to replace the former loosely-knit federation of subsidiary companies.

- Differentiation in recruitment. Career paths are being divided into clerical work force; supervisory/junior managerial; and the 'high potential' senior managerial élite. Opportunity for movement into a higher tier must none the less be kept open, to ensure that talent is not lost due to absolute rigidity in the system.

● Widespread use of formalised assessment techniques will be necessary to sharpen the recruitment and developmental processes.

● Although the bank currently invests heavily in general management education two change are envisaged. First, such education needs to complement development more fully and thus commence at an earlier stage than hitherto.

Secondly, the programme will need to be more specifically 'tailored' to the business issues facing the bank. The broadening of specialist experience will need to be a major aim of such programmes.

● Development needs to be given back to the staff. In other words, the emphasis must move towards self-development, supported by objectively-based performance appraisal, open and participative potential assessment, and application-driven job selection processes, rather than the traditional, often secret, nomination-based systems.

● The change in the organisation of the bank to address market needs will result in increased differentiation of skills and talents required. In development terms the bank's 'traditional' view of management being built on and supported by shared knowledge bases will have to change, and be replaced by a differentiated style.

● Perceptions of clearing bank careers will need to be changed. Increasingly people will need to be recruited on a high performance, high reward basis; but not necessarily for a full career life span.

● The traditional attitudes to professional qualifications need to be changed. This shift will not relate to the qualifications *per se*, but rather to their indication of aspiration and personal commitment to self-development.

● The increased focus on self-development will be underpinned by a major expansion in the application and use of technology in training, and more direct training support in the full range of interpersonal skills.

● In planning the development of the cadre of high fliers, the need for them to gain experience in *running* things, and not just doing jobs, is paramount.

Melvyn Howell sees the above points as indicating fundamental changes in the bank's development philosophy. Whilst action is occurring in all of these areas, the implicit shift in culture will take time to achieve.

Lloyds Bank

Peter Rowe, Chief Manager, Training Co-ordination, Lloyds Bank, sees the way in which the group is now organised as having paved the way for implementing necessary changes in management development thinking and practice. The bank is organised into business units, backed by a centralised group resource, which gives support in the provision and use of common resources (for example, personnel, premises and technology). The business units are enjoying greater freedom and autonomy in developing operationally, to work effectively in their differentiated markets.

These organisational arrangements create a basis for evolving a 'core' culture blended with differentiated cultures in each division. In terms of management development strategy, Peter Rowe identifies clearly the need for a range of development programmes, to cover both core and divisional requirements.

The development programme for corporate resources will be centrally controlled, and mandatory from the entry point onwards. The planned experience of corporate resources would encompass periods in selected divisions and functions designed to provide a breadth of understanding of the bank and its business.

Development programmes for divisional resources will vary, dependant upon the differing business needs within each division. It is anticipated that each division will have devolved accountability for the formulation and implementation of management development strategies to fit their needs and cultures.

The need for paths to allow individuals to cross from division to corporate programmes, and vice versa, is seen as important. This facility is necessary to provide for flexibility and optimum person/job matching.

This 'core' element of development strategy at Lloyds Bank will give rise to differing career life spans. It is anticipated that the corporate resource will tend to be a more 'traditional' career span, whilst many in the divisions will be highly marketable people with, perhaps, a greater loyalty to their specialism, or market, than to a single employer.

In moving towards this central framework for management development strategy at Lloyds Bank, Peter Rowe sees a range of related changes occurring (or identified as being necessary):

- Introduction of assessment centres, with individual assessment against defined attitude and skill requirements, is seen as important. Movement between corporate and divisional programmes would be strongly linked to assessment centres conducted perhaps, four to five times during an individual's career. It is seen as essential that assessment is a two-way process, providing information on individual aspirations, as well as skills and talents. Assessment centres will need to be supported by appropriate counselling programmes.

- The rate of change in the financial sector environment is such that Lloyds have recognised a need to combine the development of 'raw' skills with the development of individuals' ability to learn.

- Academic/professional qualifications continue to be regarded with great importance. The underlying reason for this is not the intrinsic value of the qualification, but its indication of an underlying ability to learn.

- In development programmes there is beginning to be a shift from a generic approach to the formulation of individually-tailored programmes. This is being accompanied by an increasing emphasis on self-development.

- Educational technology is already being used to deal with a wide range of knowledge and skill requirements. Increased onus on individuals, in terms of development responsibility, will need to be supported by an expansion in the use and development of educational technology.

● The changes which are emerging will give rise to a need for more open communication, in relation to career and succession planning. Succession issues will need to be openly discussed. By the time that a person is eight to ten years into their management career it is important that they are made aware, as far as possible, of their likely ultimate level, and the type of job which they will be doing.

Accompanying the changes identified above, Peter Rowe sees many of the same changes and issues identified by Melvyn Howell arising.

Citicorp Investment Bank

Malcolm Parker, Training Director of Citicorp Investment Bank, identifies the bank's culture as being strongly performance oriented. The development style is described as one of 'push and deliver'. Onus is on the individual, who will receive support if it is needed.

Given the bank's success to date, Malcolm Parker sees it as difficult to effect significant changes in development strategy. He has, however, identified a number of issues that need to be addressed, and some changes implemented, within the overall philosophy.

● In house management training programmes are now very firmly focused on business and strategic issues rather than generic skills. These programmes have a highly practical flavour, and carry an expectation that they will directly produce business-related results.

● The bank is unlikely to move to an assessment centre approach to the identification of potential. The focus will remain clearly on performance. This has consistently been found to be the most reliable indicator of potential. However, it is seen as being necessary to improve the measurement and monitoring of performance.

There will be a need to build profiles of people to provide a basis for obtaining more consistent information. Mechanisms will also need to be developed for comparing performance across units, and making better development career planning judgements.

● Career life spans, and mid-career development, are issues

currently being reviewed. The overall size of Citicorp provides plenty of scope for mid-career changes. However, the planning of careers may need better management. This will, at the end of the day, still take place within a philosophy of individual responsibility. The onus is clearly on the individual to make career choices. The bank will provide any career path, provided that the individual can justify the investment required.

Within the bank, Malcolm Parker sees change as only being actively promoted if its impact on overall performance can clearly be seen. Whilst this is a healthy check on action, it is possible to see past success and growth securing such a strong commitment to practices and policies that it becomes difficult to achieve necessary changes.

Barclays de Zoette Wedd

Barclays de Zoette Wedd is an organisation created from the merger of a merchant bank, an investment management company, a stockbroker and a stockjobber. The main initial challenge has been one of effectively integrating such diverse functions and cultures.

Given the need for integration, the organisation has not yet an established management development strategy. However, Jeffrey Hernu, the director responsible for personnel, sees management development as playing a significant role in the future development of the bank.

The core of Barclays de Zoette Wedd's development programme will be an annual graduate intake. These recruits will be a corporate resource during their first two years. They will undertake a planned programme of experience in each of the main operating divisions. At the end of the two years they will move into one of the operating units.

Like many other banks, Barclays de Zoette Wedd is seeing a separate business-unit philosophy emerging, within the umbrella of a corporate strategy.

Jeffrey Hernu recognises the significantly different cultures and skill mixes in the business units. To ensure that future corporate management needs are met, he envisages that an option for the graduate intake would be a corporate management career path. Whilst those entering operational units would be within the scope of the units' development strategy, those opting for corporate management would remain a central resource, developed under a different programme.

In looking at the formulation of an effective management development strategy, Jeffrey Hernu feels that the following points need to be considered:

● Within the operating units there will be an increasing tendency to employ specialists on a short, non-pensionable, contract basis. He sees this as a part of the inevitable move away from a 'career for life' philosophy in the financial sector.

● There is a need to accurately spot the potential of people for further development. To do this will require the introduction of assessment centres. These would be used on a regular basis; and would also provide an opportunity for people to cross over from divisional to corporate development paths.

● Achieving and maintaining effective integration of diverse functions and cultures will continue to present a major challenge. The use of joint training and education programmes, bringing together managers from different business units, is seen as a valuable aid to integration. Such programmes help to disseminate the overall corporate culture; as well as establishing operational, cross-unit networks. For example, this policy has been employed in recent sales and marketing training and resulted in positive joint selling in a number of units.

Jeffrey Hernu feels that it is vital not to lose sight of the medium- to long-term benefits of a cohesive management development strategy, whilst dealing with the short-term pressures of integration. In fact, he sees the management development process as being essential in ensuring the integration is effective and durable.

Scandinavian Bank

The Scandinavian Bank is a relatively young organisation, which does not have a strong, historical culture. David Woodward, Group Personnel Director, sees the bank as having failed in its early years to effectively develop managers, although they concentrated successfully on developing banking skills. During the last six years more attention has been given to the development of management skills.

Absence of a strong culture and tradition can be seen as an

advantage. It provides a relatively clean slate on which to produce a management development strategy designed to meet the needs of a volatile and competitive market.

The bank is rapidly moving to a separate business unit structure, with a high degree of autonomy and delegated authority in the business units.

David Woodward sees the main thrust of the management development strategy as being to create commercially-aware, flexible and innovative managers. To achieve this he sees a need to devolve responsibility at an early stage, and provide people with the experience of managing real elements of the business. He feels that this need dictates training methods which should include extensive use of projects and action learning.

In order to achieve optimum job matches, it is felt to be important to improve the quality and scope of information available on people. The need for assessment centres, improved appraisals and comprehensive personnel records is seen as vital for an effective management development programme to be implemented.

David's colleague, Geoff Ritchie, sees the major problem to be faced as that of defining the mechanism for moving from strategy and policy to implementation and action.

BUILDING SOCIETIES

Nationwide

In the Nationwide, as with many building societies, management development has been focused on the branch network. The experience gained 'in the field', and in branch management, has been seen as important in fulfilling the requirements of senior and middle management head office jobs.

Jack Rutley is the Nationwide's Management Development Manager and is responsible for formulating, and implementing, a development strategy designed to assist the society in meeting the challenges of marketing an extended range of services in a highly competitive environment.

He sees his own appointment and reporting line as signalling a major change in thinking on management development at the top of the organisation. His function has been separated from the personnel department, and he reports to an operational assistant general manager.

Whilst the main focus of management development is likely to remain in the branches, the Nationwide have moved to a two-tier recruitment pattern. Trainees are currently taken in at 'A' level standard. However, there is now a move to recruit at graduate level. Trainees undergo a formal three-year training and development programme combining technical skills, social skills, marketing and corporate investment training, with planned job experience, leading through to assistant and full branch manager appointments. Although a two-tier policy is operated, those who initially join in a clerical capacity may switch into the 'trainee' route if performance and potential assessments justify the move.

Once the formal training has been completed, on-going development of managers is achieved by a mixture of training, projects and assignments. Most managers are expected to become involved in the development and implementation of training programmes for other staff.

Job switching is seen as an important part of the society's development strategy. However, a lot of the onus is placed on the individual to indicate an interest in moving jobs.

Currently potential assessment (in terms of promotion decisions) is based on a mixture of performance appraisal data, qualifications and top management perceptions. Although formal appraisal schemes do not currently exist for senior executive staff, it is hoped that an appropriate scheme will be developed and implemented in the near future.

Jack Rutley sees a number of changes occurring in the society's development strategy. He also sees further changes being necessary:

● There is an increasing tendency to see the business developing on a separate unit basis. For example, the estate agency business would be run separately from the existing branch network. However, it is envisaged that there will be an interchange of staff between the separate business units.

● As the demands on the branches increase, together with the complexity of the business, there will be a need for a more formalised programme of management development, focused on head office.

● Increased delegation of responsibility, and authority, has led to a need to see field operations as more autonomous. This has led to a need to introduce a new level of field management; and to provide training to support changes in roles and responsibilities.

● Professionalism is a key issue at Nationwide. Greater emphasis is being placed on the importance of professional qualifications. It is envisaged that having more than one qualification will become an important indicator of the breadth that will be required by senior managers.

● The current climate is highlighting the need to introduce more formalised career and succession planning. This process is beginning with the development of skill profiles for senior management jobs.

● Achieving optimum job/people matches requires good information on past performance and identification of potential. Psychological testing has already been introduced for selection purposes; both for external recruitment and internal promotion. It is envisaged that the society will move towards the introduction and use of assessment centres as part of its overall development strategy.

Jack Rutley recognises the need for management development to extend beyond the traditional perceptions of being concerned solely with education and training. He does, however, envisage barriers to achieving the desired changes. The major barriers relate to line management perceptions and attitudes. Changing these is an important element in the overall development strategy.

Woolwich Equitable Building Society

Donald Kirkham, Chief Executive of the Woolwich Equitable Building Society, sees management development strategy as one of his major accountabilities.

At the Woolwich, the nature and extent of the changes in the market-place, and response required, are clearly recognised. To prepare managers to cope with the increased levels of competition a major educational programme is being implemented. This programme is built on the lessons from Peters and Waterman's *In Search of Excellence*, and Goldsmith and Clutterbuck's *The Winning Streak*. The programme focuses on delegation, communication and customer relations. It is designed to reinforce the overall culture, which promotes the devolution of decision-making.

The society has a policy of recruiting management trainees to meet future management needs. Like many other building societies, this part of their development programme focuses on the branch network. The Woolwich have moved from recruiting 16-year-old school-leavers as trainees, to recruiting in the 21-30 age bracket, with a high proportion of graduates.

Trainees' careers are carefully monitored. People are increasingly expected to obtain the Chartered Building Societies Institute's qualifications and a further professional qualification. Obtaining these qualifications is seen as important, in preparing them for management careers.

Although having a specific group of management trainees, Donald Kirkham is adamant that the Woolwich will not move to having an élite management cadre. All joiners are seen as potential trainees and can switch into the management trainee programme, if they demonstrate aptitude and ability.

All, except the most senior posts, are advertised internally. People are expected to be responsible for their own career progression, and to apply for jobs to broaden their experience and gain promotion.

This process is seen to be invaluable in providing staff with a clear indication of the action they need to take in order to succeed in obtaining promotion. In this way it can be said that the Woolwich place considerable emphasis on self-development.

Donald Kirkham sees this process as an important element in the society's approach to development – that of letting potential emerge.

Those who will make successful managers will be those who have shown initiative in obtaining jobs, and can back this with a clear track record of being able to perform.

The management development strategy at the Woolwich may be summarised as combining the support of central training and education with the requirement for the individual to take responsibility for his or her own career development.

Abbey National Building Society

Like Donald Kirkham of the Woolwich, Peter Birch, the Chief Executive of the Abbey National Building Society, sees management development as one of his major accountabilities. Also, like the Woolwich, the Abbey has implemented a major education programme designed to assist managers in coping with the new business environment.

The Abbey, however, differs from many other societies in its approach to organisation, and this impacts on its management development strategy. In responding to the changed market conditions the Abbey has a market linked divisional structure, which creates the climate for separate business-unit development.

The focus of the Abbey's development strategy is on succession and continuity of management. They have, for more than two years, had detailed manpower and succession plans. These include the clear identification of people with the potential to fill the top jobs. A degree of openness is present in the communication of succession plans since, through appraisals, promotions and salary increases, the 'high fliers' know who they are.

It is the business-driven manpower and succession plans which, in turn, drive the Abbey's management development strategy. This strategy currently involves the development of a cadre of people with high potential. This is being realised through extensive graduate recruitment, and the recruitment of people with good commercial experience in the 28-32 age bracket (including a number of MBA's).

Broadening of managers is a key objective in the management development strategy. This is, in part, being achieved by careful monitoring of career histories and ensuring that regular development moves are achieved (that is, every five years or so). Peter Birch has found that these moves do not have to be major ones to achieve the objectives. For example, moving branch managers to another branch, within the same geographic area, can be as beneficial as major changes.

However, at more senior levels major changes in functional accountabilities are used to broaden experience.

Assessment of past performance is found to be a good general indicator of potential within the society. The policy of moving people into a range of jobs provides performance reports and potential assessments from a variety of managers, thus increasing the reliability of any overall assessment.

Whilst the Abbey maintains training and education resources, their management development strategy is clearly focused on planned job experience. In this way Peter Birch hopes to develop a good pool of commercially-aware and broad-based managers, with the range of skills and talents necessary to meet the needs of the society.

Halifax Building Society

In the Halifax Building Society much of the management development has been focused on general trainees. These trainees receive a period of two year's concentrated training before moving into supervisory, and junior management positions, prior to moving into branch management.

Although development has focused on the branches, the society has developed a regular two-way traffic between the branches and the head-office. Crawford Laughlan, General Manager, sees this as being important in developing managers' breadth of understanding of the business, as well as increasing skills and encouraging flexible and responsive attitudes.

Crawford Laughlan sees an increasing trend to recruiting graduates as general trainees. This trend is seen as growing in importance, as the nature of the business becomes increasingly complex. However, as in many other organisations, it is felt to be essential to enable all staff with talent and aspiration to cross into the fast development track.

Although branch and head office development programmes are conducted separately, Crawford Laughlan feels that it is vital to bring the groups together for training in common skills areas, such as interpersonal skills, in order to reinforce corporate values and increase mutual understanding and support.

At the Halifax it is felt to be necessary to underpin management development with the right organisational climate. Crawford Laughlan aims to create the atmosphere of an organisation that cares about its staff, stimulates creative thought, and rewards personal contribution.

Succession and manpower planning are issues of concern right at the top of the organisation. Although manpower planning is formalised it is difficult, given the volatile environment, to define the future shape of the organisation.

INSURANCE

Legal and General Group

John Skae, General Manager (Group Resources) of the Legal and General, has been moving the company's management development strategy away from a generic skills model for over ten years. The Legal and General has been ahead of most companies in the financial sector in moving its organisation to a separate business-unit approach, with a high degree of delegated freedom to act, combined with accountability for results.

The company is now structured as a holding company with operating subsidiary companies. Given the degree of autonomy granted to the operating companies, the group functions are relatively small in terms of staff numbers.

Decentralised structures have led to management development in the operating units being strongly business-driven.

Support for the business units is provided by a highly qualified group resource. The subsidiaries' use of this resource tends to be geared towards assistance in relation to strategic business needs, rather than for 'fire fighting' activities. The use of the central resource is sustained by its success in contributing to the performance of the business.

Central control of individual subsidiaries' management development is minimal. The philosophy is that, if management in the subsidiary fails to deal with management development issues, the consequences will be felt in terms of business performance.

John Skae is responsible for overall group development and succession needs, and ensuring continuity in senior management. The numbers involved in group succession are relatively small, with the group concern being focused on around 65 positions.

At senior level person/job-matching is absolutely vital. The Legal and General are moving towards developing a clear picture of the skills and behaviours required in general management jobs. These views will be based on detailed interviews, designed to identify the critical attributes and skills required for effective job performance. This process will be built on an in-house developed system, focused on the Legal and General's needs and environment. It is believed that only such a basis has any real validity for matching and development purposes.

Once a clear picture of skills and behaviour has been produced, potential candidates for the positions will be assessed against the same categories, and appropriate person/job-matches and individual development needs identified.

For all senior managers, regular performance review is carried out against pre-established critical success factors. Individual development needs are identified in the course of the performance review. The performance focus on the appraisal process was highlighted when a new Senior Management Review programme was recently introduced. The aim of this programme is specifically designed to focus on the individual's accountabilities and managers' contributions to overall business objectives. Individual development needs in the Legal and General are identified on the basis of performance data, emerging from the Senior Management Review programme. In the future this will be supplemented by feedback from development centres (which have recently been introduced). In these centres considerable effort is put into providing feedback, and counselling participants. One of the aims of these development centres is to improve managers' self-assessment skills, which are required in improving their performance.

As a clearer picture of senior job requirements emerges, it will facilitate the identification of those staff with potential for development, and the planning of activities to prepare them for greater responsibilities in the future.

The Legal and General's approach to management development strategy is well suited to the volatile and competitive environment in the financial sector. Changes have been successful for the company; however, they have taken place over a period of time in step with development of the organisation. The anticipation of market changes, and recognition of the need for organisation and process changes to enable the company to compete and grow, is well illustrated by the Legal and General's experience.

Royal Insurance Group

Like the Legal and General, the Royal is organised on subsidiary operating company lines. The operating companies have a considerable degree of freedom and autonomy within the framework provided by overall Group strategy.

The change has been sharp in organisational terms. Harry Broomhead, Group Personnel Manager, now sees management development strategy evolving to match the organisational structure and philosophy change.

Business planning is very much objective based and the complementary management-by-objectives approach tends to underpin the management development strategy.

The Royal feels that it now has an even greater need to identify its requirements and to spot and develop 'high fliers' who will move through the organisation into operating company and Group management positions. Harry Broomhead sees a need to spot 'high fliers' for these positions at an early age (by around age 25), and to have a clear picture of those whith potential to fill senior jobs in the Group by the time they are in their mid-40s.

The changes in management development strategy will include the need to develop diverse career paths to provide for those with skills and aspirations to develop along technical routes as well as the more 'traditional' managerial routes. Harry Broomhead feels this to be important in that it requires optimum person/job-matching and can help to minimise motivational problems associated with career plateaux.

The Royal have had. for some time, a multi-tier recruitment policy. The core group, the focus of longer-term development planning, is the annual graduate intake. However, as with many other organisations, the Royal are keen to ensure that paths are left open for talented people from other tiers in the organisation to cross into the 'development stream'.

To manage the identification of potential, the Royal have introduced three levels of assessment centre. These are at approximately the same levels throughout the Group. The lower levels are conducted by the operating companies and focus on potential for promotion within the operating company. The top assessment level operates on a Group basis and is focused on potential for senior jobs in the Group. However, the Group needs to be aware of longer-term or possible longer-term candidates for these positions irrespective of the present position or age.

This network of assessment centres has to be carefully managed to ensure that people are not missed at the stage of selecting candidates and that consistent standards apply throughout the Group. Harry Broomhead sees further evolution of management development in the Royal being based on four elements, viz:

● *Audit*
  The defining of performance standards and assessment against those standards.

● *Responding*
  Ascertaining line managers needs and providing support and resources to meet those needs.

● *Employee perceptions*
Monitoring the internal climate and determining the need for action to deal with perceptions of changes in values.

● *Neutral information*
Providing line management with information relating to factual elements concerning the development of their people. The aim is to present and discuss reactions in a way which enable development decisions to be made by line management.

The use of 'neutral information' is seen as a means of securing line management involvement in management development and as a means of increasing decentralisation and delegation of accountability for development decision-making.

The Royal sees substantial value in the better use of information in development planning. They have recently introduced fourth generation computer information system for manpower data and are actively looking at methods of career control including the use of salary progression curves.

The aim is to use progressive curves to provide a systematic basis for reviewing development and identifying likely ultimate positions of people.

Harry Broomhead also sees a number of other general changes in the Group's approach to management development:

● There will be an increasing emphasis placed on self-development. This will be supported in increased use and application of educational technology in development areas.

● Whilst there will be an increasing focus on individual development plans, the Royal will retain a central group training function in some form to deal with training and education relating to common needs.

The Royal is substantially strengthening its approach to management development. There is a strong belief that the greater involvement of line management will ensure that management development makes a real contribution to needs and performance.

Allied Dunbar

Allied Dunbar is an organisation which has a successful track record of growth and innovation. It is essentially a sales-driven organisation with considerable freedom and accountability delegated to its regional and branch managers.

The organisation is results focused and, to date, its management development philosophy has been one of creating a climate and opportunities to enable talented and successful people to develop.

Peter Russell, Training and Development Manager, is responsible for building on current successes and bringing more structure into the development process, without losing the dynamism and flexibility which has contributed to success in the past.

Peter Russell has a clear view that general management positions will, in the future, have to be filled by people with a good overview of the business, and a strong commercial awareness.

The main routes to senior management have been through either branch managment, or the systems functions. Both areas are structured to focus on business needs and a broad view of the nature of the company and its markets.

The main changes in management development are likely to focus on planning.

Peter Russell sees a need to spot potential for development at an early age. Those with potential for general management should be identified in their late 20s and early 30s. As business needs become more sharply focused, the identification of potential is likely to involve a diverse range of techniques, including the introduction of assessment centres. Allied Dunbar do make quite extensive use of psychological testing to obtain optimum person/job-matches. This information, together with information on job experience and performance, will be systematically reviewed to identify potential.

Performance appraisal is already well established, with a formal annual scheme, and less formalised monthly performance reviews.

The basic appraisal programme has been supplemented with a Managerial Effectiveness programme, which involves managers being appraised by both their bosses and subordinates. This programme gives valuable information on managerial training and development needs as well as performance.

The future management development strategy will involve more detailed career planning. Once individuals with potential have been identified, the aim will be to establish jobs to which they should be moved, in order to develop the potential.

Management training at Allied Dunbar tends to be developed to support changes in organisation and systems. Peter Russell sees that it is these changes which are the main factors in bringing about changed managerial behaviour. Training is focused on helping managers to deal with their changed role.

It is seen as important that succession planning should be openly discussed. If this is not achieved the appraisal discussions are rendered meaningless.

Peter Russell envisages a continuing use of external management training courses. He sees the main function of such courses as exposing individual managers to new ideas and broader thinking. In this way the organisation can be 'seeded' with new ideas and approaches to business. The climate is such that the 'seeds' that take root, and grow, will be the ones that make a positive contribution to current or future business performance.

At Allied Dunbar changes in management development strategy will only be successful, and accepted, if their relevance to the changing needs of the business is clearly established and developed in concert with all levels of management.

Alexander Howden

Alexander Howden is one of the largest insurance broking firms in the UK. As a broking firm its organisation is one of a holding company with two operating companies, Alexander Howden Limited and Alexander Howden Re-insurance Brokers Limited. Operating divisions within the group tend to have differing cultures, based upon the type of business they broke and the markets in which they operate.

The diversity of companies within the group presents a major challenge for the Human Resource Division. Implementing a change in strategy requires careful selling of the ideas to the heads of the operating companies.

Duncan Williams, Group Training and Development Director, is looking to establish a management development strategy which effectively blends the provision of clear frameworks, with allowing people to grow in a way which suits them.

The change in the business environment is forcing the senior management to give a higher priority to management development. There is a recognition that broking firms will have a growing need for managerial skills.

The main changes in management development which are anticipated by Derek Day are:

- A need to spot potential at an early age. This will entail introducing means of assessing individual abilities and skills.

- Training and development programmes will need to focus on management principles and practices whilst developing team spirit, engendering an awareness of business realities and identifying individual effectiveness.

- Team-building programmes will be a major priority, and be designed to help individuals understand their role and realise their need to undertake self-development action.

- Line management need to become involved in the development process. This may be achieved by nominating directors of companies, within the group, to be responsible for guiding specific high fliers through their development programmes.

- Career structures are identified for both managerial and technical disciplines. At the same time individuals should be counselled in their career choice.

At Alexander Howden, Derek Day sees the need for evolutionary rather than revolutionary change in management development. He sees training as playing a major role in 'seeding' such change.

Lombard Continental

Lombard Continental is a relatively young, and small, general insurance company. It has experienced a period of fast growth and very successful performance in very difficult market conditions. The style of management has been greatly influenced by the Chief Executive. A cohesive, committed and capable senior management team is now established.

Against this background John Horner, Corporate Planning Manager, found that management development has not been an issue of major importance, as experienced managers were recruited in the company's early days. However, the organisation has now reached a stage in its growth where succession and development of managers has to be addressed.

The strategy for development in Lombard Continental is relatively simple. The organisation is small enough for the top management to have a good picture of the skills and potential of their people.

Technical excellence is a core value in the company. Development strategy is primarily aimed at ensuring those in managerial posts develop a broader understanding of the business, and its markets.

The main vehicle for management development is a training programme which is built around a core project. This project is designed to help the participants understand how an insurance company works financially, commercially and managerially.

Although the size of Lombard Continental constrains the scope and need for management development, John Horner recognises that the organisation's structure has to be regularly reviewed, to ensure that it is appropriate for meeting business goals and providing development paths and opportunities.

COMMON THEMES

Reviewing management development thinking and practice in the selected financial sector organisations provides a fairly good representation of what is happening within the sector generally.

Whilst the approaches described varied in detail, it is possible to identify the major developments in thinking common to many of them (and indeed common throughout the sector). These developments are:

● Recognition of the need for a number of career paths, covering technical as well as managerial career developments.

● Use of multi-tier recruitment with a largely graduate intake into the high flier group. However, the need to keep paths open for movement between levels is generally recognised as important.

● Formulation of differing management development strategies for separate business units is becoming common. This approach is combined with a need for a strategy for developing corporate management to be integrated with the separate unit strategies.

● Importance of job/person-matching is increasing. This is leading to the development of job and skill profiles and the recognition of the need for comprehensive information on the performance and potential of individuals. The use of assessment centres as a means of spotting potential is becoming widespread.

● Increasing formalisation of career and succession planning. The move away from generic skills development models is being accompanied by a recognition of the need to develop specific plans for individuals.

● Increasing emphasis on self-development. Individual responsibility for their own development is a common thread in many strategies. The advances in educational technology are increasing the shift in focus towards self-development activities.

● A move away from training focused on academic models of management to a focus on developing ability to learn, and on understanding the real issues facing the business.

● Academic and professional qualifications are becoming increasingly important. This trend is not geared towards the knowledge acquired, but to the evidence such qualifications provide of either commitment, ability to learn or intellectual capacity.

● Increasing openness in communication and discussion of succession plans and related issues.

● Involvement of line management is now seen as of critical importance to the success of a management development strategy. If the strategy is not business-driven, and seen as clearly contributing to performance, it is unlikely to secure the commitment of line managers.

SUMMARY

From the review of thinking and practice of the selected organisations it is clear that, in the current environment of rapid change, the 'traditional' approaches to management development do not appear to be producing the talent and skills required.

In discussions with the organisations mentioned, and others in the sector responsible for management development, doubts have been raised as to whether, without changing recruitment policies, they could ever hope to develop the managers they need.

These discussions focused attention on the following major points which need to be borne in mind when considering management development:

● Management development is far broader than purely management training and education. In many ways the reported inadequacies of management development are a result of a restricted focus. Many programmes are limited to management training and education. If there is no supporting framework then new skills will not be practised and the training activities will be historically set, rather than future looking.

● Thinking about management development tends to mirror thinking about the process and style of management in the organisation. The most common management models in many companies tend to be:

 – *Building model.* This implies a highly hierarchical and structured approach, relying heavily on each component fulfilling a predicted and defined function.
 – *Military model.* Reliance here is on organisation, understanding functions and effective leadership.

Both of these models lead to assumptions that effective training based upon historical experience will provide the skills required to replenish resources in a static structure. Both models have difficulty in coping with change, ambiguity and the need for flexibility.

● A more appropriate model for financial organisations today may well be an organic one. Here the emphasis is on creating the right climate for resources, to grow and yield the required performance.

● The emphasis on climate and environment is important for effective management development in times of change and uncertainty. Such a focus will provide the flexibility to 'grow' managers to match the differing needs of different business areas or units.

● Much management training and education fails, in that new skills and attitudes are not effectively transferred to the job. Emphasis on creating the appropriate climate can enhance the congruence between what is learned about management and how it is experienced on a day-to-day basis.

● Adults develop most effectively when they are responsible for their own learning. Given that a major need in organisations today is for people able to learn quickly, a major thrust of management development should be equipping people with the ability to learn. This, given clear communication of expectations and direction of the business, will provide the impetus for effective programmes of guided self-development.

Thus, in planning management development strategy, a company should view the subject on a broad basis, examining both climate and the range of developmental activities available. The organic model appears to offer hope of ensuring a continuing supply of talent to support future survival and growth.

8 Development Methods

In earlier chapters in this book the limitations of equating management development with management training and education have been clearly highlighted. This is not to deny that in any development programme there will be a need for some training and educational elements. However, an effective management development strategy will need to employ a range of methods, in order to meet the overall objectives.

Given the need for management development to become more business-driven, the selection of methods should be geared to identifying those which offer maximum scope for integrating development with improving job performance.

The process of development planning will result in the formulation of a range and mixture of individual and group plans. At the end of the day the final selection of methods must be determined by the nature of the development need.

Much of the available research and writing on management development focuses on methodology. However, it is becoming increasingly evident that development, to meet the requirements of the changing financial sector environment, requires a commitment to and focus on individual self-development. The rate of change and need for flexibility and speed of response tends to reduce the potential and value of company-wide, generic training and education programmes.

Achieving this shift in focus requires:

- Involvement of line management in the formulation and implementation of development plans.

- Effective communication of overall development strategy and direction.

- Development messages to be reinforced by, and integrated with, other related systems (for example, reward systems).

- The establishment of a climate which is conducive to the achievement of development objectives.

Having established that methods of development should not be selected until the needs and strategy have been clearly formulated, it is useful to review some of the methods available. This chapter provides a brief review of the range of methods currently being used for achieving management development objectives in the financial sector. A detailed description of the methods is not provided, as the focus of this book is on planning and strategy.

The aim of reviewing the methods being employed is to give an indication of planning considerations which arise at the stage of implementing a development strategy.

MANAGEMENT TRAINING AND EDUCATION

Management training and education programmes remain one of the main development methods used in the financial sector. However, the structure, style and content of these programmes, as well as the context in which they are used, is changing rapidly.

There is a major shift away from the use of generic managerial skills training for all managers. It is widely felt that this trend will continue. The use of standard business school programmes for middle management is declining.

There is a changing perception of the role of business schools. Their continued use is envisaged for senior management programmes. However, there is an increasing demand for these schools to work with individual companies to produce 'tailored' programmes, focusing on the needs and issues relating to the business.

Training programme design and content is becoming increasingly business focused. Outputs from training programmes commonly include action plans related to business issues. Participants in many programmes use 'live' situations as the basic case study material.

Malcolm Parker, of Citicorp Investment Bank, increasingly finds that the bulk of middle and senior management training programmes focus on business planning and directly result in practical action being taken to resolve major issues, or advance new developments.

One of the main management training focuses at Barclays de Zoette Wedd is to contribute to the integration of the diverse business units, and effectively disseminate the overall corporate culture and values. Jeffrey Hernu illustrated a recent example of this. Sales training aimed at junior managers resulted in practical action to more effectively market business on an integrated team basis.

The focus of management training on business issues is particularly strong at Arthur Young. In Chapter 5, Brian Chandler's 'seeding' strategy was described. This strategy is, in part, implemented by raising awareness of the need for change and generating interest and excitement, through examination of live business issues, problems, and opportunities in training 'events'.

In order to meet an increasing diversity of development needs, a number of organisations offer a wide range of management training programmes. Where this occurs, line management tend to be presented with a 'menu' from which to select training suitable to meet the development needs of their subordinates.

An alternative response to the diversity of potential needs is typified by the Legal and General. All management development training is dictated to, and develop to meet, specific business needs.

Whilst one of the main changes in the direction of management training and education is a move to a business orientation (and the real world), the other is an increased focus on the individual.

Peter Rowe, at Lloyds Bank, sees an increasing need to develop individually tailored training and development plans. This entails a move away from large-scale and common skills programmes. He also sees the content of management training, in addition to dealing with the development of specific managerial skills, concentrating more on helping people to learn how and what to learn. It is this skill which is particularly important in a highly volatile environment.

Alexander Howden is promoting technical, skills and management training programmes. This is seen as an important part of the process of developing skilled people. At Alexander Howden managerial skills and concepts are being introduced into training programmes previously seen as purely technical. This development is felt to be important to achieve, at an early stage, a change in perceptions of the technical and managerial balance in the structure of management jobs in an insurance broking environment.

To go into much more detail on the way in which the style and delivery of management training and education is changing would go beyond the intended scope of this chapter (and indeed this book). It is, however, clear that those organisations which are achieving an effective result from management training have changed their approach in the following way:

● A shift in focus from theory to practice. Concentration is on the 'real world' and on real business issues and problems relevant to managers.

● Training is driven by individual or business unit needs rather than following a pattern or coverage determined centrally.

● The training itself increasingly centres on developing individuals' abilities to learn and increasing their self-awareness, rather than teaching generic or common skills and techniques.

In a number of organisations, management training has become so business focused that it has clearly moved into a position of being accepted as an operational management activity rather than a costly peripheral one.

MANAGERIAL WORKSHOPS

As management training has become more practically based and business oriented, senior management have begun to see real benefits arising from training activities. The development needs of senior management are being met increasingly by the use of a range of managerial workshops.

These workshops tend to be concerned primarily with two areas of development, viz.:

● Team-building.

● Broadening the focus of managers and increasing their understanding of the overall nature and direction of the business.

Successful workshops tend to be structured in a way which starts by examining business issues or problems and subsequently looks at process and interpersonal areas of development.

A very common way of establishing the workshops is to bring the top management teams together to examine the organisation's strategic development. The workshop is either centred on developing a new strategic plan or considering the implementation of an established one.

The team attending the workshop work with the guidance of an internal or external consultant, whose role is to help them examine process issues and to broaden their perceptions of the implications of planning and business decisions.

Normally the first workshop will end with an agreement to continue such meetings on a regular basis and often, additionally, to establish similar workshops for subordinate teams. It is also fairly common to find that the workshops lead to the initiation of follow-up individual or joint projects. The joint cross-function projects provide an excellent basis for further team building and broadening of experience and perceptions of the business.

These workshops are very effective in generating senior management commitment to management development, both for themselves and their subordinates. They also provide an excellent basis for team-building and establishing clear corporate values.

As an alternative to business strategy, it has been found to be effective to use the formulation of management development strategy as the initial core subject for a series of these managerial workshops.

APPRAISAL

Most organisations in the financial sector have established some form of appraisal system or procedure. The appraisal process is seen, in many organisations, as an important part of the development system.

Obtaining good information on people is a critical pre-requisite of effective management development. The appraisal process provides a vehicle for obtaining information on past performance and individual career interest and aspirations.

However, appraisal has, potentially, a far wider role than this in the management development process. Used properly, appraisals should provide a good basis for examining individual development needs. The examination of past performance provides the opportunity for individuals to learn about their strengths and weaknesses and to identify action necessary to both improve performance in their current job and to develop new skills and abilities.

The discussion of future aspirations, as part of the overall appraisal review, provides an opportunity to identify the development action necessary to enable an individual to realise these aspirations.

To realise the opportunities provided by appraisal it is necessary that the system is properly designed and implemented. A lot tends to depend on how line managers operate the system in practice. Realising the potential benefits of appraisal requires careful training of line management, geared to developing their skills in conducting appraisals.

It is essential that appraisal is an open and two-way process. In examining aspirations and future career development it is necessary that managers are both constructive and realistic. All too often appraisal systems fall into disrepute because expectations are unrealistically raised.

If managers are well trained in appraisal, their involvement in the process can contribute to their own development. To conduct an effective appraisal they will need to become more aware of business performance requirements. To discuss aspirations and career development they will need to become more aware of the range of career options available, general developments in the organisation and overall management development strategy. These requirements, together with the need for good interpersonal skills, provide the basis for broadening and developing those conducting the appraisals.

A number of organisations have extended the range of appraisal discussions in terms of the people involved. Discussing performance and development needs with other managers and colleagues helps to broaden the information and development base.

In some organisations (Allied Dunbar, for example), the appraisal process has been extended to include upward appraisal by subordinates, as well as the traditional downward appraisal. This has been found to be exceedingly valuable in clearly identifying managers' development needs. Indeed, at Allied Dunbar it was the introduction of the Managerial Effectiveness programme which led to the recognition of a need to change the overall management development strategy.

ASSESSMENT CENTRES

The increasing use of assessment centres as a means of identifying potential and improving person/job-matching was reviewed in the previous chapter. However, such centres are seen by many as having a role to play in the development of both those being assessed and those making the assessments.

Commonly the assessment process is backed by counselling for those being assessed. Results and their implications are discussed with the individuals both during and after the centre. This provides a valuable way of identifying development needs and actions, and realistically reviewing career paths and options. Thus the participants should have a clear picture of their strength and weaknesses and the path to the best job match for them. The counselling discussions will also provide the individual with a greater understanding of how the organisation operates, and where it is going in terms of goals and strategy.

The material worked through in the centre (exercises, case studies, etc.) will provide developmental experience, particularly when backed with good debriefing and discussion sessions.

Assessors need to acquire a clear understanding of the purpose, structure and basis of the centre. This contributes to the assessors gaining a broader insight into the way in which the organisation is developing, and the future requirements for its effective management. In addition, assessors acquire skills in assessing performance and potential, as well as counselling and communicating in general. Overall, the training of assessors, and their involvement in conducting centres, provides an excellent development experience.

In many organisations the introduction of assessment centres is seen as being for developmental purposes as well as potential identification and job-matching. The Legal and General have separated assessment and development. They have recognised the need for (and indeed are beginning to establish) assessment centres for selection and succession purposes. They are considering the use of development centres, which are designed to help individuals identify their own development needs and undertake actions to improve current job performance. These development centres will be run over some five days, on a residential basis, in order to realise the range of developmental objectives.

When companies use assessment centres in conjunction with well-structured and run appraisal systems, they acquire an excellent data base for management development planning and action.

SELF-DEVELOPMENT

With the movement away from traditional generic skills approaches to management development has come an increasing focus on individual development needs. This shift has been accompanied by a change in perception relating to the responsibility for development. Increasingly individuals are seen as being responsible for their own development. This, in part, is a result of a broader change in culture in the sector, from a paternalistic one to a more commercially-driven one. It is also a result of the recognition of increasing diversity of skills and talents required in different parts of the organisation.

Emphasising self-development is by no means abdicating organisational responsibility for management development. In organisations where self-development is becoming more frequently used, a clear managerial role is seen. For example, at the Nationwide Building Society, Jack Rutley sees a growing need for self-development, with the management role being to help to identify needs and help the individual to structure a development programme. This is a view supported by Peter Rowe, of Lloyds Bank:

> More responsibility must devolve on individuals to manage their own development. However, management has the responsibility to help in defining objectives, providing a clear framework and identifying resources and support available to the individual.

Peter Rowe sees the use of educational technology as being important in underpinning the movement towards this growing emphasis on self-development. This is becoming an increasingly common view within the sector, particularly with the accelerating development of distance and open learning programmes, and the application of educational technology to a broader range of topics.

Companies which place emphasis on self-development tend to look at the gaining of further academic or professional qualifications as an important part of this process. The range of qualifications perceived as relevant to the needs of the business is extending. In many organisations there is an expectation that those individuals who are likely to make significant progress will have completed more than one course of professional or further academic study.

Often a philosophy of individual responsibility for development extends to include individual responsibility to seek growth in job experience, by actively applying for positions within the organisation.

At the Nationwide, the views on self-development are very wide ranging. For example, external activities such as membership of the Round Table are seen as having developmental value.

In general it seems that self-development is most effective when carefully managed. This requires the clear identification of development needs, career paths, and the value of development activities. These need to be brought together in an individual development plan, which is regularly reviewed and seen to be moving towards the achievement of realistic objectives.

PLANNED EXPERIENCE AND JOB CHANGES

In Chapter 4 the value of experience gained in performing jobs was identified as, perhaps, the major contribution to an individual's development. However, in many organisations the way in which this experience is gained remains largely unplanned. In some organisations short-term operational requirements have inhibited job changes which would provide long-term development opportunities.

Increasingly companies in the financial sector are paying more attention to the planning of job experience as a means of achieving development objectives. Frequently the output from assessment programmes, which identify development needs related to future job requirements, is converted into a plan involving the individual being move through a series of jobs which are indentified as providing the required developmental opportunities.

At Lloyds Bank they seek to ensure that job experience planning, and training activities, are carefully dovetailed. This requires a considerable amount of planning in order to ensure that the job environment is such that those having been through a training programme have the opportunity to practise and develop newly-acquired skills.

Peter Birch, of the Abbey National, sees job changes at senior levels in the organisation as a highly effective means of securing the breadth of vision necessary for senior management roles. He has been instrumental in effecting some major changes in job responsibilities. For example, the head of Abbey's legal department was moved to head the society's northern region – a job entailing responsibility for 250 branches and 2500 staff.

Whilst such major changes provide quite dramatic development opportunities, Peter Birch is keen to ensure that relatively small moves (perhaps between branches) are regularly used in order to expose managers to the experience of operating in slightly different markets and environments.

It is clear that planned experience employing horizontal job changes, as well as promotion moves, can be used to achieve a range of objectives. Experience of differing demands and environments clearly contributes to developing a breadth of understanding of the organisation and its market, as well as a degree of flexibility and adaptability.

For organisations which are grappling with the integration of diverse cultures, job rotation offers further benefits. Jeffrey Hernu, of Barclays de Zoette Wedd, sees job rotation as making an important contribution to integration in the organisation. This will result from those going through the development programme having a clearer understanding of the nature and needs of the different business units.

Within the overall framework of planned experience there is a growing recognition of the need to ensure that there are opportunities for people to acquire early managerial experience. Organisations used to regularly moving people around find that the change to a more planned approach also carries with it a need to ensure that people gain early experience of running parts of the business, as opposed to merely undertaking tasks in different units.

Whilst planned experience and job changes offer an excellent means of achieving development objectives, it is important to balance this with the needs of the business. The planning process must take account of what the individual will be expected to contribute to the job, as well as what learning will be gained from it. The plan should be performance oriented, designed to ensure that experience is gained through achievement of defined results.

Derek Day, of Alexander Howden Management and Data Services, raises an important point to be borne in mind in career and job planning. In his experience, when individuals are moved into a job they have a significant impact on the nature of the job and, indeed, change it quite dramatically depending on their experience, knowledge and skills. This underlines the need to focus the planning on the achievement of results in differing environments, rather than the mechanics of task performance.

SECONDMENTS AND ACTION LEARNING

Planned experience primarily focuses on the structuring of career paths within an organisation to ensure the development of required managerial skills to fulfil senior level roles. However, a growing number of organisations are recognising that exposure to a totally different environment can be a valuable way of developing the breadth necessary to effectively fulfil a senior managerial job. Such exposure can also be very effective in overcoming the constraints of a strong culture, as was well illustrated by the experience of Brian Chandler which was summarised in Chapter 4.

Seconding people to work in other organisations is becoming

recognised, and frequently used, as a development method. In many cases the secondments are to organisations in a totally different sector. Frequently staff are seconded to government or other public sector agencies, either operating in a related field or requiring an infusion of specific, financially-based, skills and experience.

Citicorp Investment Bank and Arthur Young are both among the growing number of financial organisations who second staff to client companies. In addition to developmental opportunities this approach has clear potential for realising the commercial benefits of closer links with clients.

As with any development method, it is important that secondments are used within a carefully planned framework. The action learning approach, pioneered by Professor R. Revans, provides a very clear framework for development involving secondment to other organisations. With action learning, the experience of working in other organisations is carefully blended with support based on a group of people undergoing a similar learning experience.

Relatively few organisations in the financial sector operate formal action learning programmes. One notable exception is Scandinavian Bank. Its Chief Executive, Garrett Bouton, is a strong advocate of this approach:

Action learning provides a unique opportunity for bankers to broaden their minds by working on some of the problems which are being experienced in other industries. It will be invaluable, too, in preparing our people for the pressures they will meet during the next decade.

Although secondments and action learning provide excellent developmental opportunities, they can cause some problems. The major problem relates to expectations. Participants in development programmes are frequently concerned with obtaining a clear picture of the purpose of the development activity, and where it will take them in terms of career path. As secondments and action learning are aimed at broadening individuals it can be difficult, at times, to relate them to a specific career move. This can be a particularly difficult problem in an uncertain and volatile environment. However, to ensure that optimum value is obtained from a secondment, it is critical to ensure that the job a person is asked to perform afterwards has sufficient scope and challenge to ensure that lessons learned may be applied in practice. It is also important to ensure that the use of secondments is accompanied by well-planned briefing and debriefing procedures.

So far secondment has been considered in terms of developing those with potential to move into more senior level jobs in the organisation. A number of financial sector companies are also using secondments to move managers out of an organisation, in order to remove career path blockages. Such moves commonly focus on managers who have plateaued, and are in a position which blocks further development of people identified as having high potential. In many cases secondment provides a solution which benefits all parties. The manager being moved is presented with a new challenge, instead of possible stagnation and frustration; the receiving organisation acquires new skills, and the company is able to more effectively implement its management development strategy.

COACHING

Interest in ensuring that people obtain the maximum developmental value from job experience has led to a growth in the use of coaching in the financial sector. This method entails the individual's immediate superior acting as a coach, and helping the individual to improve his job performance and increase the level of his skills and competence. Individuals undergo planned coaching programmes which are aimed at optimising the job-based learning, and increasing the individual's freedom to act as competence grows.

The managers who act as the coach undergo training, which explains the coaching process and develops coaching skills. Involvement of managers in a coaching role provides valuable personal development for them. Those companies which have introduced coaching programmes have found them to be effective in developing managerial skills in both the individuals being coached and the managers doing the coaching.

The introduction of coaching programmes can increase the benefits obtained from appraisal programmes. Regular reviews of performance, identification of gaps, and development of action plans associated with coaching, tend to ensure that appraisal becomes a regularly used and integral part of the managerial process.

As organisations in the financial sector place increasing emphasis on individually-based development programmes and self-development, so they are recognising the need to provide individuals with an appropriate framework and support. The introduction of coaching programmes can go a long way towards providing this support.

PROJECTS

The need to balance business needs with development needs is very effectively met by involving managers in specific, business-related, projects. In the financial sector extensive use is made of projects as vehicles for management development. Uncertainty and rapid change in the financial markets give rise to many opportunities to establish short-term projects, to deal with business requirements. For example, the rapid expansion in financial product range gives rise to a need for feasibility studies, to determine whether or not an organisation should develop a particular product. This sort of study provides the basis for a project or assignment which also provides real developmental opportunities.

Projects provide a wide range of possible developmental opportunities:

● *Individual projects*

An individually-based project provides the opportunity to broaden an individual's understanding of the business and its environment. Such projects also provide opportunities to acquire new skills and develop knowledge, whilst contributing positively and specifically to the business.

● *Team projects*

Involving people in project teams provides a means of developing early managerial experience for the project leaders, without having to disrupt the core business organisation.

For those not leading the project, the opportunities of working with people from other parts of the organisation provides a good basis for developing an increased breadth of understanding of the business, as well as experience of team-working, and the acquisition of skills and knowledge associated with the specific project.

In general, projects enable people to experience greater accountability for decisions, and authority and freedom to act, than may be possible within the structure of line jobs within the organisation. Performance delivered during the project can provide valuable insights into the individual's ability to handle increased responsibility, and operate in a more flexible and ambiguous environment where rules and precedents are not clearly established.

It is important that projects are meaningful and not merely established as a developmental tool. Projects should be seen to have clear, business-related objectives and be structured in a way which focuses on the achievement of results.

When integrated into the overall management development strategy, it is increasingly common to find projects linked with individual development plans and coaching programmes. In this way the full benefits of the project-based development may be realised.

Opportunities provided by a project for people to 'run things', rather than undertake tasks, is seen as a major benefit. Ensuring that the most is made of this opportunity is well illustrated by practice at Scandinavian Bank. Here people on the management development programme undertake projects at an early stage. These projects have clear objectives, and results have to be achieved within specified budgets. Currently projects are related to the mainstream business and operations of the bank. However, very serious consideration is being given to giving 'trainees' a brief to establish and run a small business, in any sector the individual chooses. A budget will be made available, and returns required on the investment agreed at the outset. In this way individuals would be exposed to the whole range of managerial functions, from planning to implementation and control, and acquire a high degree of commercial awareness. This increased commercial awareness is perceived as a critical attribute for future senior management in the bank.

In smaller organisations the use of projects is proving particularly valuable. The size of these companies often limits the scope for planned career development built on job rotation. Thus project-based work provides a crucial way of broadening the experience of people, in order to prepare them for more senior management positions. At Lombard Continental use is made of projects for just these reasons. However, the approach has a further benefit. John Horner (Corporate Planning Manager, Lombard Continental) has identified a range of organisational and systems issues which need to be addressed in the company. The size of the company prohibits the employment of full-time specialists to deal with these issues. Thus they have become the basis for projects, which have often arisen from planning conferences attended by senior managers. In this way both developmental and business objectives are effectively achieved. Examples of projects used in this way in Lombard Continental include identification of manpower planning requirements and the establishment of appropriate systems and procedures, reviewing marketing methods, and the effectiveness of establishing expense control procedures.

At Barclays de Zoette Wedd, Jeffrey Hernu sees projects as a means of providing a basis for contributing to the effective integration of diverse cultures in the different business units. He is keen to establish cross-functional projects as a means of exposing managers from different parts of the organisation to alternative cultures and environments. There is felt to be plenty of scope for such projects, particularly in areas such as business development and marketing. Given the increasing tendency of the customers to seek integrated solutions to their problems, there is an excellent opportunity to assemble cross-functional project teams to address related marketing and product development issues.

As the financial sector moves to greater product diversity and reduced standardisation, the stability of many jobs will decrease. With this will come an increasing degree of fluidity in organisation structure. Such an environment will make it more difficult to develop long-term career path planning, based on planned experience acquired through a range of jobs. The use of project-based development, in a planned and carefully managed way, will provide a more flexible means of achieving developmental objectives.

TASK FORCES

Organisations such as Citicorp Investment Bank, at one end of the spectrum, and Lombard Continental, at the other, are making use of 'task forces' to deal with a range of business and organisational issues.

In some ways it is difficult to draw a clear distinction between a 'task force' and a project team. One approach to making the distinction is to focus on the nature of the work to be carried out by each group. The project team tend to work to a clear brief in terms of objectives and time frame. The task force, on the other hand, is concerned with resolving a transient problem or issue. The time frame and objective is often less clear at the outset.

The task force is often organised to work on a full-time basis to resolve the problem, whereas the project team may only work together on a part-time basis.

Task forces provide many of the same development opportunities as project groups. However, they frequently provide greater opportunities for developing experience of working at different levels, and in different roles, in an organisational structure. The task force may well have a formalised organisation structure, providing a number of opportunities for people to experience managerial roles without having to achieve the promotion necessary to gain such experience within the mainstream structure.

Recognition of the additional contribution and responsibility resulting from membership of a task force, in some cases, carries financial benefits as well as developmental ones. At Lombard Continental those taking part in task force activities receive financial rewards to recognise their contribution, and reinforce the business-driven nature of the approach. This is seen as clearly signalling the organisation's view that development and business performance are inextricably linked.

CHANGING JOB STRUCTURE AND ORGANISATION STRUCTURE

Changes in the financial sector environment are placing pressures on companies' existing organisation and job structures. The rate of change has led to frequent job and organisation structure changes. The level of long-term structural stability is likely to decrease as the market demands greater responsiveness and flexibility from companies.

Against this background, development based upon planned experience set within a stable view of jobs and organisational structure becomes increasingly difficult to realise.

A number of organisations in the financial sector have recognised the problems of building development strategy around existing job and organisation structures. In these organisations changes in the structure of responsibilities of key jobs and, in some cases, changes in organisational structure, are used as means of achieving development objectives. The movement towards identification of separate business units, and increased devolution of accountability, provides a good opportunity to use job and organisational structure changes for development as well as commercial purposes.

The job of the head of a business unit may be structured along the lines of a general manager of a subsidiary company. This will provide the opportunity for the encumbent to develop a more commercial perspective than would have been possible in a job designed as a head of function or department.

The use of changes to job and organisational structure also provides the opportunity to create positions enabling those with potential to gain managerial responsibility at an earlier stage in their career.

The use of changes in organisational structure seems to be particularly successful where companies are diversifying and introducing new products or tackling new market segments.

Changing job and organisation structures can be an expensive method of development, unless such changes are carefully linked with business needs and objectives. It is important to establish at an early stage that structures are likely to change further for business or development reasons. In the finance sector there is a firmly established expectation of stability in structures. Unless the need for flexibility and change is clearly communicated it may well be perceived as managerial indecision or even incompetence.

In smaller organisations changes in job structure are seen as an essential part of developing the breadth necessary to move into senior managerial roles. John Horner, of Lombard Continental, has seen such an approach used very successfully in his company. He quotes as an example a change in the structure of a senior marketing job designed to help develop a broader appreciation of the overall management of the business. In this case the marketing manager's accountabilities were extended to encompass responsibility for the company's regional operations. In this way he gained important insights into the conflicting demands of business acquisition and the delivery of the service once business was on the books.

DISCUSSION GROUPS

In the Halifax Building Society Crawford Laughlan makes use of discussion groups as developmental vehicles. These groups meet on a regular basis to discuss management and economic topics. The groups are set up with briefing sessions to put the discussions into a developmental context.

The aim of these groups is to encourage participants to think broadly and creatively about business-related issues. The groups are required to make presentations to senior management on the issues discussed. It is felt that these presentations provide a focus to the discussions, as well as creating an opportunity for practising and developing communication skills.

SUMMARY

This chapter has, by no means, provided a comprehensive review of management development methods employed in the financial sector.

What it has done is to highlight the most widely-used methods and indicated some of the thinking evolving in relation to methods of achieving developmental objectives.

Whilst management training and education programmes remain the most commonly used method of development, the nature and structure of these programmes is rapidly becoming much more practically focused, and more clearly related to the company's business strategy and objectives.

This focus on the real world, the demands of actual jobs and the nature and strategy of the business is a common thread throughout the other methods of development. Apart from training and education, the other development methods and approaches examined were:

- Managerial workshops
- Appraisal
- Assessment centres
- Self-development programmes
- Planned experience and job changes
- Secondments and action learning
- Coaching
- Projects
- Task forces
- Changing job structures and organisation structure
- Discussion groups

It is clear within the financial sector that, for management development to be a credible process, the selection of methods must be determined by their ability to contribute to both developmental and business needs and objectives.

There is no single development method which will meet all requirements. The diversity of methods available underlines the importance of careful planning in the formulation and implementation of management development strategy.

As business in the financial sector becomes increasingly complex, so will the need for strategic planning of management development grow. With this growth will come a need for a more commercially-oriented and creative approach to developing programmes and identifying new development methods.

9 All Systems Go

Throughout the previous chapters, in discussing management development strategy it has been necessary to consider other personnel-related policies or procedures, in order to obtain a clear overall picture.

The changing environment in the financial sector is not only giving rise to needs for new managerial skills and talents, but also for new attitudes and behaviour. Thus, in establishing a management development strategy, it is necessary to review all of the systems which are likely to affect the behaviour of managers.

This chapter examines the need for an integrated approach to formulating management development strategy, and examines the main systems which impact on the development process.

AN INTEGRATED APPROACH

Irving Borwick, of the Management Education Centre, has highlighted in his research and consulting work that many approaches to management development and changing managerial behaviour fail to achieve the desired results. This failure is put down to the fact that most methods of development focus on the individual, or groups of individuals, and ignore their involvement and interaction with the systems surrounding their jobs.

Irving Borwick's approach to development and change is based on systems theory. It assumes that all behaviour is integrated and inter-related as part of a system. Intervention for development or change must be made at the system level rather than at the individual level. Using this approach he has had a considerable degree of success in helping organisations to manage change and resolve problems of managerial behaviour, which have been resistant to approaches focused on the individual.

The need for an integrated approach to formulating management development strategy is an illustration of a systems approach to development.

All too often the development strategy fails to achieve the desired results, because its focus is on training as the major means of achieving results. The approach tends to follow the sequence:

● Identification of business need.

● Definition of required change in managerial role and/or behaviour.

● Development and implementation of training to bring about change in behaviour to meet need.

● Change fails to occur (or fails to be sufficient) to meet identified need.

It is normally only when the desired result has not been achieved by training that other actions are considered. At this stage some 'tinkering' with related systems, impacting on managerial behaviour, occurs.

The problem with this sequence is that the messages communicated via the training are not supported by those communicated by other systems.

The approach implied by the work of Irving Borwick, and succesfully used in the finance sector by companies such as Allied Dunbar, follows a different sequence:

● Identification of business need.

● Definition of required change in managerial role and/or behaviour.

● Change in systems impacting on behaviour, to achieve desired shift and develop required behaviour.

● Development and implementation of training to support change in systems.

This approach results in managers receiving supporting messages from all of the systems which impact on their behaviour.

In practice there are a large number of systems which impact on managerial behaviour. These are shown diagrammatically in Figure 9.1.

In the process of formulating a management development strategy it is necessary to determine the degree of congruity or dissonance between the objectives and messages of the strategy and those conveyed by the related systems.

Clearly change will be most effectively achieved if all systems carry identical messages. In practice this can be extremely difficult to achieve. It is necessary to identify the degree of impact which

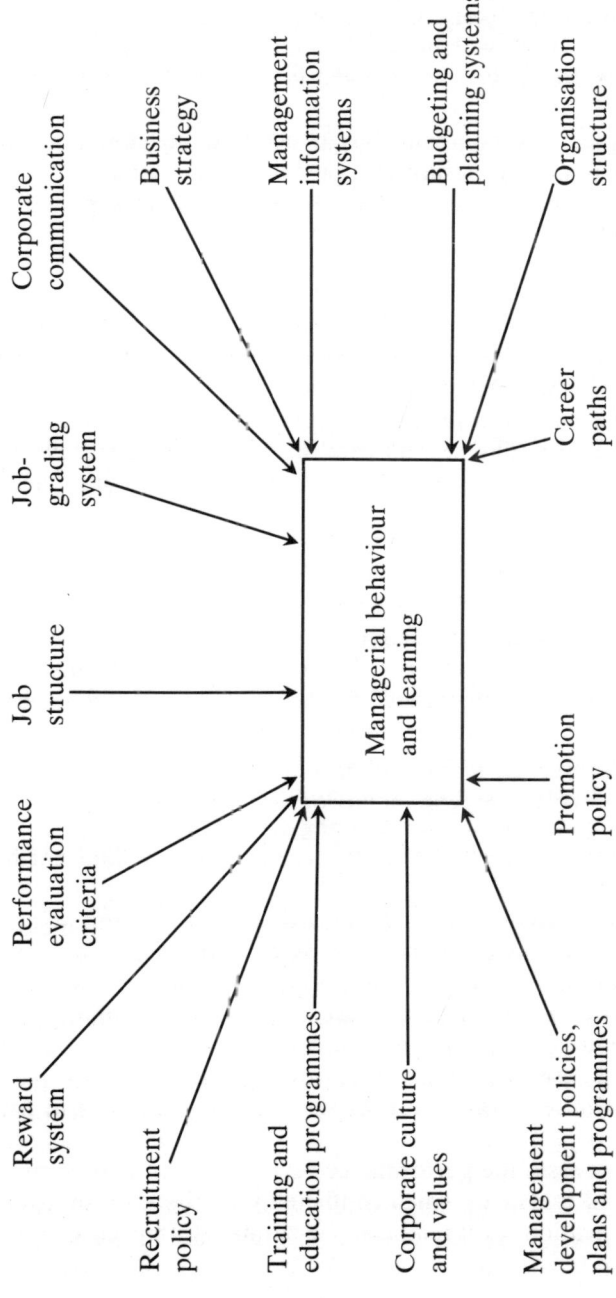

Figure 9.1   Systems impacting on managerial behaviour

different systems are likely to have on the desired behaviour being sought. This analysis will help to establish priorities, in terms of which systems do need to be changed in order to realise the results required.

For example, if a company has a need to develop innovative behaviour, it is vital to ensure that performance evaluation criteria, and reward systems, are changed in a way that supports this development.

Two cases

The significance and impact of an integrated approach to development strategy can be illustrated by considering two cases. The first relates to the application of a training-led approach, which did not achieve the desired results. The second case shows how results have been effectively achieved using an integrated, systems-based approach.

Case 1
A retail bank had identified a need to change the role of its branch managers. To compete effectively in the changing financial markets it was felt necessary to change managers from lenders and administrators to marketeers. Their effective performance of marketing and selling functions was recognised as being critical to the future development and growth of the retail business.

To bring about this change a major training initiative, backed by communication programmes, was launched. All branch managers went through an intensive sales training programme.

On completion of the exercise the required results had not been achieved.

Subsequent analysis clearly demonstrated that the initiative had failed to take account of the range of systems that had a bearing on the behaviour of the branch managers. Performance reviews and evaluation criteria continued to place considerable emphasis on the quality of lending and effective implementation of administrative procedures. These performance reviews played a major part in determining the level of reward of the branch manager and future promotions.

Thus, in this case, the performance review, reward and promotion systems carried messages which conflicted with those of the training and communication programmes. In terms of impacting on the behaviour of the managers the message from the performance-related systems were the strongest.

It was only when the bank began to change the performance evaluation criteria for its branch managers that they began to see a change in behaviour and increased focus on marketing and selling in the branches.

It is probable that, in this case, the initial focus on the performance-related systems would have reduced the need for such an intensive training and communication programme. It is certain that the desired results would have been achieved much more rapidly.

Case 2

Allied Dunbar is one of the UK's leading life assurance companies. It has an extensive branch network. As the market has changed, the company has recognised a need to become a complete financial services organisation. This has meant an extension of the range of products which have to be marketed through the branches.

At the same time increasing competition has resulted in a need to pay a greater attention to the total profitability of branches, rather than focusing primarily on sales volumes.

To achieve these business needs, the company recognised that the behaviour of the branch managers would have to be changed.

The role of the branch manager has been redefined to include accountability for an extended product range, and for overall branch profitability. This newly-defined role, together with the reasons for change and overall strategy, has been communicated to the branch managers. Communication has been backed by a change to the performance evaluation criteria and structure of the managers' remuneration package

The managers moved to operate in the new role. As they became familiar with the demands of the redefined job they were able to identify the support they required, in order to achieve targets and meet objectives. Training activities to support this change were subsequently developed in response to demand from the managers.

In this case, using intervention in systems to communicate the desired change in managerial behaviour, has been successful. In addition to realising the specific objectives of this change, the approach has reinforced the company's core culture and values which relate to a focus on results, combined with a high degree of devolution of decision-making and freedom to act. The company has defined both the direction of change and results required. Managers have had the freedom to determine how they will achieve these results in their branch, and what support they require.

From these two cases it is clear that a management development strategy which is not integrated with the systems impacting on managerial behaviour, is unlikely to succeed in meeting either developmental objectives or business needs.

This requirement for an integrated strategy is fast becoming recognised in the financial sector. The way in which the interaction between the development system and other human resource systems is being considered in the sector is summarised in the following pages.

REWARD SYSTEMS

The build up to 'Big Bang' led to an increasing focus on the level and structure of remuneration packages in the financial sector. It became increasingly clear that the reward system is a powerful means of communicating both the relative importance of skills and behaviour, and the organisation's need for results and performance. In the words of Malcolm Parker of Citicorp Investment Bank:

Remuneration policy is one of the main factors in influencing and directing change in managerial behaviour.

Equally, at Allied Dunbar, Peter Russell is convinced that:

The most significant action we can take, in terms of changing the behaviour of our managers, is to adapt the structure of the remuneration package.

In general, throughout the sector there is a recognition that reward will have to be more directly related to performance as organisations become more results-conscious in the competitive environment. Equally there is a growing recognition that reward policy will have to become an integral part of developmental planning.

As the focus of development shifts towards increasing business awareness and commercial skills, the reward policy will need to be more clearly related to profitability in order to underline the messages.

Changes in remuneration practice in the sector is taking the form of greater use of cash bonuses, and incentives related to both organisational and business unit performance and profitability.

Recognition of the need for differing development strategies for business units and 'corporate resources' carries a need to consider how reward policy should be used to support such strategies.

A two-programme approach (that is divisional or functional, and corporate programmes) needs to be supported by a clear reward policy. Divisional resources would need to be fitted in with the remuneration practice operating in each division. Corporate resources will have to follow a different earnings pattern which is likely to be more heavily geared to longer-term rewards.

Within this framework there is a need to sharpen the relationship between performance and reward, and also to ensure that succession needs are backed by a policy which balances the recognition of the value of experience and service. Overall this points to the evolution of a diverse suite of reward policies requiring careful management. The nature of the market will also mean that the reward policies will have to be highly competitive, in order to both attract and retain the skills the organisation requires in order to suceed.

In Chapter 7, the Royal's use of salary progression curves illustrates a structured recognition of the links between salary, performance and career progression. The feedback of this information to line managers helps to increase their awareness of the interrelationships, and take them into account in developmental planning.

This process of increasing line management awareness of the impact of remuneration policy on development is becoming more widespread in the sector. Devolution of accountability to business-unit levels is, in a number of organisations, being accompanied by a devolution of authority for reward management. When this happens, line managers need to be educated to understand the relationship between reward policies and practices and development strategy, in order to be able to effectively achieve succession and development objectives.

The movement towards separate business-unit strategies is increasing the degree to which managers are targeted with real profit accountabilities. To underpin the development of the skills necessary to operate on this basis, it is important to develop bonuses and incentives linked to profitability as part of the remuneration policy. When this happens, the remuneration policy becomes an effective means of disseminating and reinforcing more commercially- and market-related corporate cultures and value systems.

Derek Day, of Alexander Howden Management and Data Services, sees a need to match reward policy to the needs for developing future skills. In general, people will be drawn towards areas offering high potential rewards. Within insurance broking firms this has, in the past, led to an emphasis on technical, broking and marketing skills being developed; as these were the ones being most highly rewarded. Given the need to change the balance of managerial and technical skills, there is a need to change the reward policy in a way which increases the recognition of the contribution of management skills to business performance.

At Citicorp Investment Bank, Malcolm Parker sees a need to change the remuneration policies in order to secure real commitment to a shift in focus from individual performance to team performance. He feels that communication of intention, and training activities, will fail to achieve a change in behaviour while the reward policy focuses on individual performance.

In addition to considering overall reward policy as an integral part of management development strategy, a number of organisations are now considering direct linkages of reward to development activities. For example, the move to self-development backed by distance learning will impose demands on the personal time of people. In some organisations, which are following this route, consideration is being given to providing direct financial incentives for successful completion of programmes of study.

At Lombard Continental the task force approach to development is reinforced by payment of bonuses related to the achievement of task force project objectives. This direct linkage of financial rewards to development activities is felt to underpin the organisation's commitment to the development strategy.

In looking to use reward policy to communicate new corporate values, and reinforce development strategy, a number of organisations are finding that the high benefits element in financial sector reward packages can constrain the degree to which changes may be effectively implemented. The pensions position and practice, in particular, is seen as a major constraint in changing 'cradle to grave' career perceptions and encouraging greater mobility and flexibility. There is a general expectation that the need for changing career cycle practice and expectations, in response to market needs, will increase the pressure for greater portability of pensions and thus mobility of people.

Overall, in the financial sector reward systems are being more widely integrated with management development strategy. This integration is largely due to the increasing requirement to relate practices to business- and market-driven needs. Both reward and development systems are moving towards supporting diversified business-unit requirements. The challenge for the management of both systems is to effectively cope with the co-ordination of diverse practice in order to achieve corporate goals and objectives. In the same way that a single central management development programme can no longer meet the needs of an organisation in an increasingly diverse market, a single central remuneration policy is no longer appropriate, and no longer reflects market conditions and organisational performance needs.

PERFORMANCE EVALUATION

In Chapter 8, the links between performance appraisal systems and management development strategy were considered. Many organisations have recognised the need to change appraisal systems in order to support a revised management development strategy. These changes have been geared towards separating appraisal of performance from assessment of potential. At the same time, appraisal of performance has become more objectively based and more closely related to business needs, issues and results.

Given that there is a need for management development strategy to be more business-driven, and related to overall corporate strategy, so there is a need for performance appraisal systems to be similarly oriented. If this change does not occur the effectiveness of the development strategy will be impaired. As performance appraisal impacts on both reward and performance, the messages which it carries will have a far greater impact on managerial behaviour than those carried by other systems.

The impact of congruent messages from related systems is very high in terms of managerial behaviour. If the development system emphasises the need for business-driven development, and is backed by a performance evaluation system which rewards performance, the possibility of bringing about a change in managerial behaviour is high.

In the preceding section, the movement towards sharpening the relationship between performance and reward was highlighted. A further development in the financial sector is movement towards ensuring that the performance evaluation criteria are relevant to business needs and objectives. Peter Rowe, of Lloyds Bank, sees a need for a shift in the focus of performance evaluation criteria within banks:

In banking there has always been a conflict between entrepreneurship and prudence. In the UK, absence of bad debts, loan security and good branch routines have been major performance criteria applied to many managerial jobs. This will have to change, with greater emphasis on market related criteria. Such a change will have considerable knock-on effects on training needs, performance appraisal and related systems.

Many organisations in the financial sector are changing their performance evaluation criteria. The shift is from quality-based to objective-based criteria. Increasingly the evaluation criteria are emerging from annual business plans, and the performance appraisal system is becoming more effectively integrated into the business planning system. Melvyn Howell, of Midland Bank, sees a clear need to link performance and business planning:

A virtuous circle may be created within which the strategy of the organisation signals the demands which individuals must rise to in the future; its operating plan component sets the current year's objectives; and the performance management system should cement the two.

The need for developing increasing commercial awareness in managers is being underpinned, in a number of organisations, by performance evaluation criteria placing greater emphasis on profitability, rather than volume-based indicators of performance.

The change described in relation to both performance and reward systems in the financial sector indicate that a number of organisations have a good basis on which to build an integrated management development strategy.

RECRUITMENT AND PROMOTION

Recruitment and promotion policies and practices clearly have a very direct impact on the nature and effectiveness of management development strategy.

These 'systems' need to be fully integrated with the development system.

There has, as has already been mentioned, traditionally been a preponderance of 'grow our own' recruitment policies in the sector. These have often been based upon the view that, if a good 'pool' of high calibre people are recruited, the desired talents and skills should emerge after a period of time.

If the management development strategy is geared to developing skills and talents related to a clear understanding of the future needs of the business, then recruitment policy and criteria have to become much more sharply focused.

Equally, if a company wishes to move from a policy of 'buying in skills as and when needed' to one of developing talent internally, recruitment criteria may well have to be scaled up to provide appropriate people to be developed.

Many companies have moved to a two-tier recruitment policy. Having made this move, they are better placed to evolve recruitment criteria which are more sharply focused on future business needs, and may be more effectively integrated with the development system.

In the same way that recruitment policy has to be integrated with the development system, so does promotion policy. Unless promotion decisions are clearly linked to current and future business needs, the effectiveness of the management development strategy is seriously undermined. For example, if promotion is based upon, say, service and adherence to rules and procedures, and the development strategy is focused on performance, the promotion 'system' will convey a conflicting message. In such a case the promotion 'system' would exert the more powerful influence on managerial behaviour.

Within the financial sector, the move towards greater use of assessment centres, and increasing focus on establishing effective people/job-matching, provides a good basis for ensuring that the promotion 'system' supports the management development strategy.

ORGANISATION DESIGN

The aim of many management development strategies is to ensure that people obtain early managerial experience. This aim can be extremely difficult to achieve if the organisation structure is such as to present few opportunities for relevant experience to be gained.

External pressures are having a considerable impact on organisation design in the financial sector. However, it is important to examine organisation design as part of the process of planning management development strategy. If the organisation design cannot be modified, the strategy must be evolved within such a constraint. On the other hand, to formulate a really effective strategy, there should be the facility to establish a dynamic relationship between the strategy and organisation design. Such a relationship may readily be established, provided that both 'systems' are clearly focused on business-driven needs and issues.

The importance of organisation design in the formulation of development strategy was highlighted by Garrett Bouton (Chief Executive of Scandinavian Bank) in an address to the International Conference on Bank Training in 1986:

One of the skills which is frequently lacking in human resource functions is organisation design. With the rapid changes taking place in our industry this will become a more important feature in our organisations. If you plan your development process to match the corporate strategy of the organisation, and you accept that individual experiential learning is becoming a more important requirement, you must have an environment in which people are allowed to have responsibility and grow as a result of the experience.

Thus management development strategy cannot be effective unless it is clearly integrated with the structure of the organisation.

JOB EVALUATION AND GRADING SYSTEMS

Traditionally financial sector organisations (particularly the larger ones) have been characterised by formal grading structures. These have tended to be consistently applied throughout the organisation, and often reflected the strongly hierarchical nature of the organisation structure.

The principles on which evaluation systems have been established have tended to communicate values concerned with clarity, consistency and equity. Criteria are frequently established to determine the movement between one grade and another; systems tend to be bound by rules and/or guidelines which constrain frequent or significant change. Grading structures often create a perception of incremental career progression through grades, frequently on a single grade movement basis.

These evaluation and grading systems underpin the organisation's salary policy and structure.

In a climate, in which flexibility and rapid change are key characteristics, these 'traditional' grading systems can act as a major constraint. The increasing need to compete aggressively for specific skills has put enormous pressure on existing grading and evaluation systems, and is calling their value into question.

Additionally, as organisations are moving to a separate business-unit philosophy, the validity of an organisation-wide grading structure is being questioned.

Many organisations within the sector are reviewing, and changing, their grading and evaluation systems. If not totally changing them, they are certainly excluding specific jobs or business units from their coverage.

In formulating a management development strategy it is essential that the impact of the grading and evaluation system on managerial behaviour is carefully considered. This is one area in which the system may well have to be changed in order to achieve developmental objectives.

Already a number of companies which have moved to a 'multi-tier' career path policy and a separate business-unit philosophy, have changed their grading and evaluation systems. Commonly a strong grading structure is retained in the 'processing' part of the organisation, whilst a far more flexible approach is adopted for 'high fliers', key managers and senior staff in business units.

To an extent, as the movement to strongly performance-driven reward systems grows, the need for grading and evaluation systems becomes less critical.

CHANGING ASSUMPTIONS AND APPROACH

The need for an approach to management development which effectively integrates the systems impacting on managerial behaviour, leads to a framework which differs significantly from that associated with the approaches commonly employed.

Many approaches to management development are characterised by the following framework:

- The focus is the individual, or groups of individuals with similar needs.

- Managerial behaviour may be isolated and dealt with individually.

- Problems result from individual behaviour, attitudes and performance.

- The reasons for attitudes and opinions are more important than the actual behaviour.

- The aim of development is to help the individual gain insights which will lead to a change in behaviour.

- The process of development will bring about changes in attitudes.

- The methods used will focus on seeking solutions to individual or common group problems.

A systems approach to development, as described by Irving Borwick and used in a number of financial organisations, work within a framework where:

- The focus is the system, and its interrelationship with other systems.

- Behaviour occurs in the context of a system.

- Problems are a result of a failure in the system, or its relationship with other systems.

- Actual behaviour is more important than underlying attitudes and opinions.

- The aim of development is to realign relations in order to improve, or change, systems functioning.

- To bring about changes in systems functioning, it is not necessary to change individual attitudes.

– The methods used will focus on strategic interventions impacting on systems influencing performance.

The significance of this shift in the framework, surrounding the systems approach to management development, is the broadening of the issues which need to be taken into account in formulating development strategy.

SUMMARY

Successful formulation and implementation of management development strategy is increasingly dependent upon an integrated approach, which identifies the changes needed in all systems impacting on managerial behaviour in order to achieve developmental objectives. In the process of planning, the systems impacting on managerial behaviour need to be reviewed to determine their degree of congruence or dissonance with the objectives, and messages, of the development plans and activities.

In practice, it may not be possible to impact on, or change, all systems affecting managerial behaviour. However, their effect on behaviour may be viewed on a priority basis, and action taken to ensure that the main systems support and reinforce the development more innovative behaviour in its managers it would be critical to ensure that the performance evaluation criteria and rewards systems are structured to support this development.

In the financial sector changes in development strategy in a number of organisations are being accompanied by changes in:

● Remuneration and reward systems.
● Performance appraisal systems and evaluation criteria.
● Recruitment and promotion policies.
● Organisation structure and design.
● Job evaluation and grading systems.

The pressures leading to many of these changes have resulted from the same environmental changes underlying the movement in thinking on management development. In some organisations an integrated change has resulted from coincidence rather than planning. In future, however, it is important that management development proceeds on a planned integrated basis.

The scope of such an integrated approach significantly changes the breadth and complexity of the management development role in an organisation. It is this change in role that is examined in the following chapter.

10 Changing Accountabilities for Development

The preceding chapters have built up a picture which points to significant changes being needed, and indeed occurring, in approaches to management development strategy formulation and implementation in the financial sector.

This chapter examines how these changes are being, and need to be, managed in practice. In particular, the differing contributions made by different levels of management, and the respective roles of personnel and management development specialists are examined.

COMMITMENT FROM THE TOP

As was made clear in Chapter 3, the far-reaching scope of a management development strategy, designed to make an effective contribution to the business needs of an organisation in a competitive and volatile environment, requires clear and firm commitment from the top of the company. This commitment, in practice, needs to go beyond agreement to strategic direction and allocation of resources. Real commitment entails involvement in both overall planning and in implementation of plans, as they impact on senior level jobs.

Peter Rowe, of Lloyds Bank, points out that, particularly in a large and well-established organisation, management development strategy needs to be driven from the top. In the absence of such commitment he feels that it will be impossible to overcome inevitable line management resistance to the change associated with the implementation of a business-driven development strategy.

Commitment from the top is particularly important in ensuring that developmental objectives are not thwarted by parochial, and frequently short-term, operational requirements.

At the Woolwich Equitable Building Society, Donald Kirkham (Chief Executive) sees management development as one of his key accountabilities. He is actively involved in initiating changes in development strategy, to ensure that the society will continue to

187

compete effectively in the current and future competitive markets. He is also very actively involved in detailed succession planning and assessment of candidates for key senior posts, together with other members of his executive. Involvement with development strategy, and consideration of related issues, is perceived as being as important to the continued success of the business as areas such as corporate and strategic planning. This commitment is seen as signalling the importance of the subject to other levels of management, thereby securing their support and commitment.

Like Donald Kirkham, Peter Birch (Chief Executive, Abbey National) feels that management development must be a Chief Executive accountability if it is to be successful.

As well as taking accountability for overall strategy, Peter Birch reviews potential and development issues with all of his direct reports. He feels that his approach to the development of those reporting to him should mirror the approach embodied in the strategy. In this way, appropriate levels of commitment and enthusiasm may be generated at all levels of management.

Peter Birch has become actively involved in detailed development issues in respect of Abbey National's senior management. He feels that if the Chief Executive is not seen to be actively involved in the development process, people will begin to question its value and importance.

The views and comments quoted above tend to be reflected in most organisations, in the financial sector, where management development is seen as a significant element in effective business strategies.

In those organisations in the sector where there is no clear commitment from the top, it is far more difficult to implement a cohesive management development strategy. In the absence of such commitment, it is unlikely that line management will attach appropriate priority to development actions and issues.

CORPORATE VERSUS BUSINESS-UNIT DEVELOPMENT

For those companies which are following a separate business-unit strategy, differing needs for management development arise at corporate and business-unit levels. These differing needs give rise to differing roles and responsibilities for management development at different levels in the organisation.

Within these organisations it is common to find a senior group, or corporate manager, having accountability for the overall management development strategy, and for ensuring that group or corporate development and succession needs are met effectively.

At the Legal and General, John Skae (General Manager, Group Resources) has overall accountability for the Group's management development strategy, and is accountable for ensuring that senior level succession and continuity requirements are met.

Each subsidiary company is accountable for its own operational management development strategy. However, group needs may override those of the subsidiary company if it is necessary to move a manager out and into a different role to fulfil group succession requirements.

With this devolution of accountability has come a devolution of development resources.

At group level, a specialist management development resource is maintained to assist the general manager in group planning and strategy matters, and to be available to work with operating company management as required.

The devolution of management development accountability has been a part of the process of general decentralisation of human resource management. Each operating company has its own personnel department and the larger ones have specialist trainers. Line management normally look to Group Resources to advise on, or provide, management training. They would also certainly look to this resource for support in relation to senior management development.

At the Royal, Harry Broomhead (Group Personnel Manager) has a similar accountability for management development to that of John Skae. At the group level he is accountable for succession and manpower planning input to the corporate plan.

When the structure of the Royal Group was changed, personnel matters were largely decentralised to the personnel function of operating companies, to enable them to relate more effectively to the needs of business units. The aim is to provide the senior management in the operating companies with an effective resource to help them deal with manpower and management development accountabilities.

Derek Day, Managing Director of Alexander Howden Management and Data Services, is responsible for group succession planning. He is also responsible for providing management in the operating companies with support and guidance, and ensuring that management development actually happens.

In fulfilling this role, Derek Day understands the need to educate senior management to win their commitment to responsibility for staff development in their company. He sees this as representing a major change in perception. Although operating companies enjoy a great deal of autonomy in business management and decision-making, many human resource policies and practices remain centralised (for example, reward management). He feels that the 'education' process related to the development accountability needs to focus on its relationship to business performance, and be supported by a change in the role and style of the central human resource function.

The same distinction between corporate and business-unit accountabilities for management development is seen by Jeffrey Hernu of Barclays de Zoette Wedd. He sees the devolution of accountability for management development as an important element in the overall process of integrating diverse businesses into a cohesive group. Effectively communicating a distinction between group, or corporate, and business-unit needs, is seen as important if the bank is to avoid the problems of business-unit managers resisting change which could be perceived as diminishing their freedom to act. Jeffrey Hernu feels that a highly-centralised accountability for management development strategy planning and implementation would be difficult to fulfil in an organisation encompassing diverse business units.

LINE MANAGEMENT INVOLVEMENT

There is widespread agreement that, in future, management development strategy will need to involve line management more extensively, in both planning and implementation, than has been the case in the past.

Clear devolution of accountability in separate business units is clearly a major step in securing this involvement. However, irrespective of organisation strategy, there is a need for line managers to be committed to, and take ownership of, management development within their areas of operation.

The driving force for change in management development is coming from business requirements. Melvyn Howell, of Midland

Bank, sees this as changing the way in which development is planned and managed in an organisation:

> The new approach to management development will not be driven by personnel specialists. Instead it will be driven by line management's need to respond to the pressures of the market-place.

To secure line management involvement will, in many organisations, entail bringing about a change of attitudes and perceptions. Peter Rowe, of Lloyds Bank, anticipates that these changes may take time due to the impact of previous approaches to development:

> For a long time managers have not participated sufficiently in development decisions. Therefore they tend to lack perspective and awareness of needs. We must overcome the problems of their commitment being influenced by a too parochial and short-term perspective.

The process of securing line management involvement and commitment needs to be carefully managed. It is important that the devolution of accountability is supported by effective communication, education, advice and guidance. It is essential that the way in which the accountability is fulfilled is carefully monitored, and that the change in ownership is not perceived as abdication of responsibility by central functions.

Active involvement of line management at the planning stage is an important first step in obtaining their commitment. Involvement in implementation stages, such as acting as assessors in assessment centre programmes, helps to underpin commitment and broaden managers' perceptions of the nature, scope and importance of management development.

Once it had been clearly established that the management development strategy arises from business needs, and is designed to contribute to business performance, it becomes easier to secure line management support. When managers see that development programmes and methods do not relate to academic models, but rather to the real world, they will become more willing to be involved in the process.

REPORTING AND ORGANISATION

Even though the Chief Executive is increasingly taking overall accountability for management development, and line managers becoming increasingly involved, there remains a need to have people involved in the management of the process, and provision of resources. The question arises as to where in the organisation these people should be placed, and to whom should they report. In addition there is a question as to whether or not new skills need to be brought into the organisation to deal with management development issues.

Within the financial sector a wide range of practices are encountered in relation to the positioning, structure and reporting of management development posts.

In organisations such as the Abbey National and Woolwich Equitable Building Societies the co-ordination and implementation of management development is an accountability of the personnel function. Specialist expertise tends to be acquired by planned use of consultants or other external resources. In-house resources, in the personnel function, ultimately take over the delivery of training and education programmes.

The Royal Insurance Group also have management development established as part of the personnel function. However, the principle of decentralisation is followed in that the Group Personnel Department takes the 'top slice', that is, that concerned with succession to the most senior positions in the Group, whereas other management development work is carried out on a decentralised basis by the operating companies. The Group Personnel Department does retain a capacity to offer occasional help to operating companies in a number of personnel areas from time to time.

The Legal and General, as was mentioned earlier, maintains a specialist management development group resource. The decentralised personnel managers have access to the group resources, as do operational managers, to provide support, advice and guidance in relation to operating company requirements.

Nationwide Building Society have separated management development from the personnel function. They are in the process of building expertise in management development. The head of their management development function, Jack Rutley, reports to an operational general manager. This reporting relationship has been deliberately established to underpin the philosophy that management development is business-driven and impacts on business performance.

Allied Dunbar is a company which has management development both as a part of the personnel function and as part of the operating divisions. The need for a development strategy as part of the overall business strategy led to their recruiting in a number of specialists and positioning them in a way which reinforced the business orientation of the function.

In many organisations the decision to separate management development from the existing personnel and training functions results from perceptions of personnel as being unrelated to business issues. The nature of the role and performance of personnel functions has, in many organisations, resulted in its receiving a 'bad press'. In looking at development strategy it has frequently been felt necessary to distance development functions and specialists from the personnel function. However, it has also been recognised that the role of the personnel function will have to change. The way in which this change will occur is explored later in this chapter.

The driving force for positioning development functions within the organisation is the need for results which contribute to the achievement of the business objectives. The problems with structure, and selection of people for personnel and training functions in many financial sector organisations (and the need to change this) were highlighted by Garrett Bouton of Scandinavian Bank:

> In some organisations, the people responsible for development and training are isolated from the workplace and from the planning process. They became educationalists, and experts at designing cost effective courses. They don't know where the company is going or how it plans to get there. Success for them is turning out groups of happy people with a reasonable degree of technical or managerial competence – within budget.
>
> Other, more enlightened, organisations take their trainers and developers from the line for a period of two to three years. In this way they keep the training and development function in tune with what is happening in the real world. These people can contribute a number of ideas to in-house programmes and then return to the line with a wider skills base.
>
> In the very enlightened organisation the head of development reports to a very senior manager, who is himself a part of the corporate planning process of the organisation.

Although positioning and reporting relationships of management development specialists are key to the success of the function, the way in which their role is structured and executed is equally important.

Derek Day, of Alexander Howden, is quite clear on the nature of the Group Training and Development Director's role:

> The role of the management development specialist is that if a facilitator. Those who make management development work are the people who are responsible for the business.

He also feels that the role is proactive, rather than reactive. It is concerned with helping directors and senior managers learn how to manage.

In general the role of the management development specialist may be viewed as being concerned with:

● The organising and co-ordination of both planning and implementation of strategy.

● Acting as a catalyst to line management in the process of identifying needs, and exploring methods of meeting them.

● Providing information, guidance and direct assistance in formulating and delivering development programmes.

● Communicating the organisation's overall strategy, and gaining support and commitment from line management. Also ensuring that line management views are recognised and understood.

● Reviewing and evaluating the effectiveness of development plans, providing feedback and identifying gaps and needs for further action.

A management development strategy is most effective when it becomes accepted as an integral aspect of the management of the business. The management development function, wherever it is positioned in the organisation, is most effective when the advice, guidance and support is of such a level and nature that line managers actively seek it out as an input to the resolution of business problems.

CHANGING ROLE OF THE PERSONNEL FUNCTION

In examining the positioning of a management development function, within the framework of an integrated strategy, many organisations in the financial sector have begun to reappraise the role of the personnel function.

Increasingly the scope of management development strategy is such that it provides an overall human resource management strategy. If such strategies are to be effectively implemented, it is essential that those responsible for human resource policy, and implementation, fulfil a role which is compatible with a business-driven strategy. In many organisations this implies a change in the nature and role of the personnel function.

In general there is an acceptance that the role of personnel functions will need to change from that of administration, control and 'policing' of personnel practice to that of providing a significant contribution to business performance.

To do this there is a need for personnel people to get closer to line management, and to work with them to resolve business issues and meet business needs. In many organisations this process has been initiated by decentralising the personnel function and placing personnel people in operating companies, business units or divisions. Examples of this change were given in the preceding section.

The role of personnel is seen by Harry Broomhead (Group Personnel Manager, Royal Insurance) as needing to change. Obviously the role needs to be proactive. It is also necessary for personnel people to be aware of the nature and needs of the business. However, many personnel people in the past have been proactive and have been able to relate to the needs of the business fully. What is now needed is, perhaps, an even greater sense of 'closeness' to line management, and a relentless search for ways in which personnel practices can 'add value' to their operations. Part of this is certainly the better use of information.

Personnel management is a broad area and there is a wide range of personnel skills. Whilst it is difficult to say exactly where the emphasis is going to lie in the future, Harry Broomhead believes that resourcing and employee commitment will continue to be major areas. This will entail commenting and advising on resourcing issues in response to line managers' views on business needs and plans.

He believes that there will be an increasing tendency for personnel people to become generalists, moving in and out of the function for spells, rather than pursuing personnel work as a whole career. Organisationally they are likely to be so positioned – at group level, at operating company level and within operating companies, so that they are clearly seen as part of operational management teams. The need for specialists within personnel functions will tend to decline to a level of one or two corporately positioned and one or two within each major operating company.

In many ways it is essential to bring about this change in the personnel role in order to enable a new management development strategy to be implemented. In the eyes of many managers, management development is traditionally seen as a function of personnel. At the same time their perceptions of the personnel function are of one which attempts to control and limit their freedom to act, rather than contribute to business performance. Against this background it is important that, certainly in relation to management development, the structure of communication and implementation of strategy should clearly position the personnel function in a support and resource role rather than a direct management one.

Dissemination of policy from senior management to the line directly through the personnel function often results in a failure to achieve objectives. This arises due to a mixture of bureaucratising the policy, to ensure policing and control may be implemented; and line management resistance, due to their perceptions of the personnel function.

To ensure that policies work, and to underpin the changing role of the personnel function, policy communication should be directly from senior to line management, with personnel people identified as a resource. It is then up to the personnel people to get close to line management and demonstrate that they have value to add as a resource in policy implementation. This framework is one which will help to ensure that policy is translated into action.

INTEGRATION WITH BUSINESS PLANNING

Throughout this book the need for management development strategy to be integrated with business planning has been emphasised. The need surfaces again in considering the positioning of the management development function in the organisation.

In a number of organisations in the financial sector there is a recognition that the person with accountability for management development should be in a position to input to the business planning process.

Garrett Bouton, of Scandinavian Bank, emphasises the importance of positioning development people in a way which ensures that an effective integration with the planning process is achieved:

These days, more than ever before, the planning process is significant and vital within banking. Because of the environmental changes taking place, it will be an even more dynamic process with constant changes as we update and improve our services and products and also take advantage of opportunities which may present themselves. If people development and training is to be a proactive part of this process then the people responsible for it must be very close to, if not part of, the organisation's planning process.

This requirement is clearly met when the chief executive is actively involved in formulation and implementation of management development strategy. It is important to support this by ensuring that management development specialists have direct reporting, and access, to management involved in corporate planning.

BARRIERS AND PROBLEMS

Changing the role of the personnel function, ensuring the effective distribution of management development accountabilities and implementing a changed management development strategy will not be without its difficulties. Achieving desired results will necessitate overcoming a number of barriers and dealing with a range of problems. The major barriers and problems identified in the financial sector are:

● *Line management perceptions of the need for management development*

Traditional approaches to development have often been seen as peripheral to business needs. This means that many line managers will not readily see how management development activity will be relevant to their business, and to achieving their objectives in a challenging environment.

● *Parochial and short-term focus of line managers*

Development focuses on the longer-term needs of an organisation and relates to an overall picture of the business. Line managers are frequently more concerned with the 'here and now' and the needs of their immediate area of responsibility. The broadening of their focus presents a major challenge which, in itself, should be part of the overall development strategy.

● *Line management perceptions of the personnel function*

In many organisations line managers perceive personnel functions as bureaucratic, and a barrier to achieving their own objectives. It will take time to gain our confidence in moving to a more proactive, supportive and business-driven personnel role.

● *Changing skills within the personnel and development functions*

In moving personnel management into the line, in the role of a resource to managers, it will be necessary to ensure that personnel people are equipped with appropriate skills. These staff will need to develop a greater business awareness, together with influencing and persuasion skills in order to be able to win line management confidence and operate effectively.

● *Misunderstandings relating to the purpose and nature of changes*

Great care needs to be taken in communicating the aims of any changed development strategy and personnel role. A move to devolve personnel and development accountability may easily be misread as a dismantling of the personnel function, rather than a change in the way in which it operates.

It is important to ensure that line management are clear that devolved accountability carries with it a requirement to effectively fulfil such accountability. If they are aware that their performance of this area will be evaluated alongside other accountabilities, they are more likely to seek to use the resources provided by decentralised personnel functions.

The barriers and challenges primarily relate to line management perceptions and attitudes. However, perceptual and attitudinal problems may also arise amongst personnel staff. They may see their role being diluted, or resist a change from a specialist to a generalist focus. Once again clear communication, and participation in decision-making, will help to overcome these barriers.

SUMMARY

It is clear that moving towards a business-driven approach to management development requires rethinking the role of the personnel function, and the positioning of management development specialists in the organisation.

Whether management development is a part of the personnel function, or has a separate reporting line, it is clear that top level commitment and involvement is necessary to underpin a successful strategy.

It is also clear that the specialist staff involved in management development must develop a broad perspective of the business and its needs to be able to demonstrate an ability to support and contribute to the achievement of business objectives.

In practice the formulation, implementation and control of management development is frequently an accountability exercised by an organisation's human resource function.

Unfortunately the planning and implementation, when seen as the sole responsibility of the human resource function, tends to result in a highly bureaucratic and static system, characterised by unwieldy documentation. Objectives are frequently not achieved, due to the inflexibility of the system and lack of line management commitment.

To ensure that continuity and development needs are effectively met it is vital that line management are actively involved in the formulation and implementation of policy.

Once the overall strategy has been developed, ensuring that it is implemented and works effectively should be a line management responsibility.

It may be possible to develop an overall framework in which each business area is responsible for formulating its own continuity and development plans, which would be designed to mesh with group or corporate plans.

Even if significant responsibility for continuity and development is devolved, there will remain a need for some form of central human resource management involvement.

The key areas of accountability to be exercised by the central function would include:

● Overall responsibility for communication, direction and co-ordination of the process of planning and development of policy.

● Organisation-wide analysis of data relating to the planning and development process, and involvement in identification of group needs.

- Provision of a co-ordinating service and 'clearing house' facility in relation to developmental transfers and resourcing of projects.

- Provision of advice and guidance to line management in the formulation of plans, design of development activities and implementation of programmes. Also involvement as a potential resource in the implementation of programmes.

- Development and implementation of core management training and education programmes to meet group needs.

- Development and implementation of management workshops and seminars to meet specifically identified needs.

- Development and implementation of policies and practice to support management development strategy (for example, recruitment, career planning).

- Implementation of changes to related personnel systems and procedures (for example, performance evaluation system), and monitoring changes to ensure desired results achieved.

To fulfil these accountabilities the key managers in the human resource function will need to operate in a highly consultative way. They should act as an internal consultant. Change should be achieved based upon the provision of good quality professional guidance and the ability to relate the 'know how' to a range of business and operational requirements.

In addition to a high level of professional personnel and training knowledge, the key managers will need to have a good understanding of the organisation and its business, and be able to develop and apply process consultation skills.

11 A Framework for Action

This book has set out to examine how management development strategy is being formulated, and implemented, in the financial sector. It has also examined changes in the perceptions and practices of management development. The need has been established for change, in many organisations, to enable them to survive and flourish in a volatile and fiercely competitive environment.

Within the financial sector thinking varies widely about management development strategy and approaches to its implementation. A number of companies have recognised the importance of management development in their overall business and strategic planning. In other cases there has been no real recognition of any need to shift from their traditional approaches to development.

Where the need for a change in management development strategy has been recognised, the drive for such change has frequently emanated from the Chief Executive. In practice senior level commitment to, and involvement in, the process plays a major role in ensuring that necessary changes occur.

There is a fairly widespread realisation that, in order to make a real and positive contribution to business performance, management development must shift from being concerned with generic views of managerial processes and skills, to being more firmly rooted in the reality of the business.

The range of systems impacting on the development of managers is diverse and requires an integrated approach to the formulation of development strategy. A number of organisations, committed to management development as a means of improving business performance, have recognised and acted upon this need.

In determining a strategy, and implementing a management development plan, there are a considerable number of issues and variables to be taken into account.

In spite of the range of variables there do appear to be a number which are clearly fundamental to the success of a management development strategy. These are:

● The need to involve line managers in both the planning and implementation phases.

● A requirement to examine development in a broad context and not to perceive it purely as management training and education.

● The necessity to focus clearly on future business requirements and the implications of these, in terms of organisation, job structure, managerial style and person/job-matching.

● The need to ensure that action, in the areas of management development, is supported by the messages conveyed by related systems impacting on the behaviour of managers.

The nature of the current business environment, and its rate of change and uncertainty, leads to a requirement for a flexible and responsive approach to management development.

Action will be more effective if it is focused on establishing an organic programme capable of growth and evolution, rather than a highly mechanical and tightly-defined one.

The remainder of this chapter outlines a possible action framework for the formulation and implementation of a management development strategy appropriate to the needs of many financial sector organisations. The proposed framework is offered as a suggestion to be fed into the overall planning process and to provide a stimulus to further discussion. Clearly it will not be appropriate, in total, in all organisations. However, the underlying approach will, to some extent, be relevant to most organisations in the financial sector.

OBJECTIVES

The objectives of the action framework described may be summarised as:

● Identification of the likely future structure of the organisation, structure of jobs and organisation climate, so that potential job holders may be effectively developed to meet performance requirements.

● Identification of the organisation's succession requirements, and establishment of action programmes, to ensure an adequate supply of suitably skilled people is available to meet future needs.

● Identification of managerial skills and talents which will be required to ensure effective implementation of the organisation's medium- to long-term strategy.

● Development of a clear picture of the current range of managerial skills and potential, and identification of future gaps which will need to be filled.

● Provision of a basis for structuring and implementing training, development, education programmes and changes to related systems to make the most effective use of resources and contribute to achievement of business goals.

OVERALL APPROACH AND ORGANISATION

Given the need to secure line management involvement, the starting point for any action programme should be the establishment of a management development project team.

This team should have members drawn from senior management, representing a number of the key business areas, together with senior management from the personnel functions.

The size of an organisation and its managerial population could well preclude the one project team from handling the whole task. In addition different business areas are likely to have differing needs. Thus, under the main project team a number of individual business-unit project teams may need to be established, with membership drawn from senior line management in that area and supported by a senior member of the personnel function.

The top level project team would be responsible for overall strategy and reviewing overall corporate needs encompassing, say, the top three levels of management.

In addition to the project teams the personnel function would need to establish a team with the brief to:

● Carry out specific reviews. For example, reviewing the structure and content of existing training and reviewing performance evaluation systems.
● Co-ordinate the work of the project teams and communication relating to the strategy.

The overall organisation of the project could well be as shown in Figure 11.1:

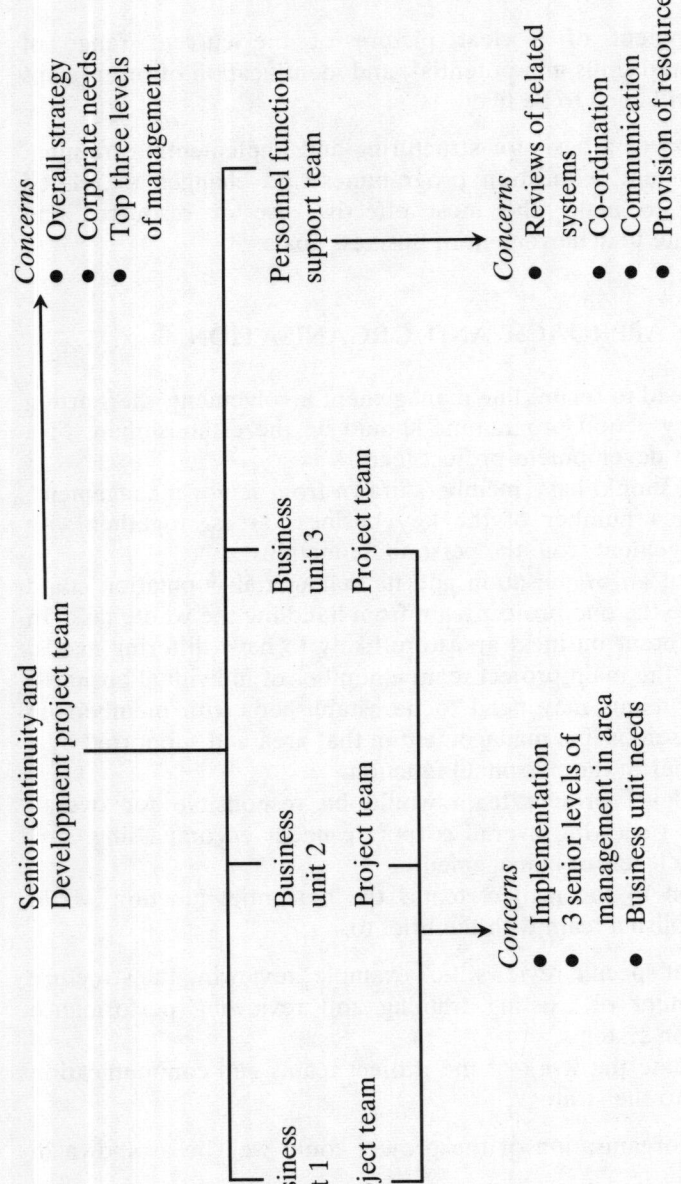

Figure 11.1 Organisation of the project

Although this approach is relatively heavy in its use of senior management resources, it does have the following advantages:

- The level of involvement will lead to commitment to the programme.

- The involvement in the project teams, in itself, provides developmental opportunities for the participants.

- The investment increases the chances of effective management development occurring.

- There is a clear communication of the organisation's commitment to the process.

STRUCTURE

Within this overall approach to development planning, the framework which the project teams would operate may well be as follows:

1. Review business strategy

Identify current and projected corporate strategy.
Identify current and projected strategy for separate business units.
Identify current and projected problems, issues, barriers and forces for change.
This would apply to the senior project team. The second level project teams would focus on the business unit strategy.

2. Establish current organisation structure

Identify and review corporate structure.
Identify and review structure of business units.
The second level project teams would focus on the business units only.

3. Identify future structure

Using material from 1 and 2 discuss and identify likely future organisation structures.

4. Job analysis and current jobs

Select a sample of key jobs to represent the current structures.
Interview job holders and produce job description covering purpose,
dimensions, principal accountabilities, structure and reporting.
Discuss the impact of changes identified on job structure.
Identify problems and performance barriers.
The personnel department team may provide the resources to
produce the key job descriptions.

5. Job analysis and future jobs

Based on information from 2, 3 and 4 develop outline job profiles
for future jobs.
Test and agree future job description outlines.

6. Knowledge and skills analysis

Using information from stages 4 and 5 identify, for each job,
knowledge and skill requirements.

7. Performance and success criteria

For a sample of current jobs identify, and agree, performance
measures and success criteria.
Relate success criteria for movement through current structures.
Identify and agree likely performance and success criteria for future
jobs.
Identify and agree likely criteria for movement through future
structures.

8. Career histories

Obtain career histories for encumbents of selected sample of jobs.
Discuss and identify match between career histories and achievement
of performance and success criteria in each job held.
Identify gaps, problems and issues raised.

9. Skill inventory

For sample encumbents obtain performance data, assessment data, details of training and education.
Obtain superior assessment of potential.
Obtain self-assessments.
Obtain aspirations and interests.
Develop skills inventory.
At this stage use is also likely to be made of assessment centres.

10. Matching

Match the skills inventory with the knowledge and skills analysis.
Identify current and potential matches and gaps.
Match actual with projected career histories.
Identify required career paths.
Match performance and success criteria.
Identify experience requirements.

11. Development planning

At this stage the range of information obtained is reviewed to identify group, and individual, development needs.
The team would also have available the results of the personnel teams' reviews of existing training programmes and changes needed in support systems (for example, performance evaluation).
The team would produce:

● Analysis of common development needs.
● Career path – experience plans.
● Identification of action needed in relation to other systems impacting on development.
● Group and individual development plans.
● Succession and recruitment requirements.
● Identification of appropriate range of developed activities.

12. Briefing

On a cascading basis the project teams could conduct workshops with line managers to discuss conclusions, agree on their validity and agree on implementation plans.

In terms of timing, it is likely that the senior team would conduct their work first and develop a briefing workshop for the second level teams.

Additionally, individuals briefing sessions would be required on a manager subordinate basis to review individual development plans.

The personnel function would be responsible for developing, resourcing and implementing training programmes identified during the project. They would also be responsible for co-ordinating and assisting with the implementation of development activities.

Once the initial project has been completed there would be a requirement for periodic reviews (probably annually). The co-ordination of the review process and monitoring of implementation would be a personnel function responsibility.

Adopting the approach outlined will require the commitment of time and resources. It will clearly involve more people in large organisations. However, their need for change may well be greater and have to be underpinned by the level of involvement and participation indicated.

CONCLUSION

The changes which are taking place within the financial sector are fundamental and have far-reaching consequences. The process of change is likely to continue and result in a volatile market in which it becomes increasingly difficult for organisations to continue to operate as they have done in the past and still enjoy profitable growth.

An effective management development strategy, which is business-driven, and integrated with other systems and the organisation's planning processes, is increasingly becoming a critical element in relation to future success in a tough environment.

The pervasive nature of change in approaches to the formulation and implementation of management development strategy, as described in this book, requires commitment, effort and resources. However, this investment in people is as important as investment in technology and products, if an organisation is going to survive and succeed in the future financial sector environment.

References

- *Excellence in Banking* by Steven I. Davis (Macmillan, 1985).
- *How Chief Executives Succeed* by T. Margerison (MCB Publications, 1980).
- *In Search of Excellence* by Thomas J. Peters and Robert H. Waterman Jr. (Harper and Row, 1982).
- *Journal of European Industrial Training* by W. Braddick (MCB University Press, July 1984).
- 'The Managerial Menopause' be John Davies and Yvonne Deigham (*Personnel Management*, March 1986).
- 'Should Management Development be a Three Way Contract?' by J. M. Harries (*Training and Development Journal*, July 1986).
- *Tomorrow's Men Today* by Andrew and Valerie Stewart (Institute of Personnel Management, 1981).
- *The Winning Streak* by W. Goldsmith and D. Clutterbuck (Penguin, 1985).

Index